THE MANOR OF WRITTLE

The development of a royal manor in Essex
c.1086–*c*.1500

THE
MANOR OF WRITTLE

The development of a royal manor in Essex,
c.1086–c.1500

BY

K. C. NEWTON

County Archivist of Essex

1897

PHILLIMORE
London and Chichester

1970

Published by
PHILLIMORE & Co., LTD.,
Shopwyke Hall, Chichester, Sussex

SBN 900592 082

Printed by Stephen Austin and Sons Limited,
Caxton Hill, Hertford.

PREFACE

The Little Domesday Book reveals Writtle as one of the largest manors, both in population and territory, in Essex, the importance of which was enhanced by its being royal demesne. This importance is assessed in relation to the County, the Hundred of Chelmsford and its constituent manors, particularly Chelmsford. Factors which led to the subsequent decline of Writtle and the rise of Chelmsford to the status of County town in the 12th and 13th centuries are considered.

By the 14th century the Manor had become an inward-looking community, jealous of outside interference, for the expression of which its rights and privileges provided the necessary apparatus. It is with aspects of its history as a largely exclusive estate, community and franchise that the remainder of this study is concerned.

The topography of the Manor is examined by deliberately taking the demesne and tenants' lands separately, so that the emergence of an individualistic enclosed system of cultivation out of an original common-field pattern of farming may be postulated and its subsequent development in a formerly heavily forested area traced. The tenurial structure and the working of the demesne on the 'classical' model are considered. There follows a study of the closely related subjects of the change to leasing the demesne, heavy decline in acreage under cultivation and population and the fragmentation of holdings in the 14th and 15th centuries. Finally, the jealous attitude towards interference by outside organs of justice and the continuing importance of the manor courts as a steadying influence in an era of change are looked at in greater detail.

ACKNOWLEDGEMENTS

In any work based on research one is constantly aware of the debt which one owes to those who have worked in a similar field and have made their learning available in print or typescript: this is, I hope, sufficiently acknowledged in the footnotes. I am particularly indebted to Miss H. E. P. Grieve, B.E.M., B.A., who with customary generosity made available to me the results of her as yet unpublished history of Chelmsford High Street. To Mr. F. G. Emmison, M.B.E., F.S.A., F.R.Hist.S., the former County Archivist of Essex, and to Mr. A. C. Edwards, M.A., the former County History Adviser, I am grateful for their constant encouragement. I also wish to thank those who have generously made available to the public their archives for study, in particular the Right Hon. Lord Petre, Lord of the Manor of Writtle.

K. C. Newton

CONTENTS

ILLUSTRATIONS

I

BEFORE AND AFTER DOMESDAY

The evidence of pre-Conquest settlement at Writtle is fragmentary and, apart from that recorded in the Little Domesday Book for the later Saxon period, rests wholly on archaeological finds and what is suggested by a study of place-names.

A Neolithic hammerhead was found in about 1881 in a yard;[1] Bronze Age and Iron Age remains have been uncovered in a field close to the parish boundary with Chelmsford[2] and others of the latter period on the site of the former manorhouse.[3] With singularly little evidence some early writers attempted to identify Writtle as the site of the Roman settlements of *Caesaromagus* and *Canonium,* but archaeological evidence now places the former certainly in the Moulsham area of Chelmsford and the latter probably at Kelvedon.[4] Discovery of two burial urns in 1840 and other finds suggest, however, that there was a minor settlement in Roman times.[5] Possible traces of a Roman road leading to Little Waltham have recently been found.[6]

After the Roman period the record—documentary or three-dimensional—is silent until the compilation of Domesday Book in 1086. The name, Writtle, suggests that it was not among the earliest Saxon settlements, for it derives from *Writolaburna,* the Old English name of the River Wid which winds its way across the extreme south-east corner of the manor.[7] The great Survey shows

---

[1] *Transactions* of the Essex Field Club, vol. ii, p. 30. It was almost certainly brought in from the fields.

[2] *Victoria County History, Essex,* vol. iii (1963), p. 203.

[3] See p. 11 below.

[4] *V.C.H., Essex,* vol. iii, pp. 203, 149.

[5] *V.C.H., Essex,* vol. iii, p. 203. A field on the eastern boundary of the manor was called 'Erneborweslond' in the early 15th century (see, for example, court roll, E.R.O., D/DP M235), later corrupted to Earthenboroughs Croft (*e.g.* in court book, D/DP M1465).

[6] *Ibid.*

[7] Writolaburna signifies 'the bubbling, purling stream'. (Ekwall, *English River Names,* 1928, quoted by P. H. Reaney, *Place-Names of Essex,* (English Place-Name Society, vol. xii. 1935), p. 278).

1

that the manor of Writtle had been part of the possessions of Harold before the Conquest, but implies that earlier it had formed part of the Crown lands. In the main entry relating to Writtle, a hide of land held by the Bishop of Hereford is said to have belonged to the King's fee (*in feudo regis*); when this information is repeated under 'The Land of the Bishop of Hereford', the hide is described as having belonged to Harold's fee (*feudo Haroldi*).[8] The conclusion that Writtle was royal demesne before 1066 is reinforced by the render of 10 nights' 'feorm' given in Domesday and by the evidence of later manorial records.[9]

The incomplete picture of the manor given in Domesday is at first view similar to that of many other Essex manors, a wholly agricultural community with no free tenantry.[10] The statistics also present those problems of interpretation which abound as soon as any folio of the Survey is considered. The most striking aspect of the figures is the size of the estate in terms of its hidage, population and value. Of the 440 or so places mentioned in the Essex Domesday[11] only 10 were rated with greater hidages in 1066, 11 in 1086.[12] Disregarding Colchester and Maldon, the only places in the county which were in any sense towns, Barking alone had a comparable population immediately before the Conquest and a significantly larger one in 1086.[13] Neither Barking nor any of the other manors with larger hidages had a greater value. Barking was valued at £80 both in 1066 and 1086, though at the latter date 'the French' appraised it at £100, a sum equal to that for Writtle. Waltham Abbey was valued at £63 in 1086 (only £36 in 1066), Southminster at but £16 (£24), Hatfield Broad Oak at £60, though £80 was received annually from the lease (£36),

8   Domesday Book, ii, ff. 5b, 26.

9   It is evident that all Crown lands in Essex had become part of the possessions of Harold. For a discussion of this by J. H. Round, see *V.C.H., Essex*, vol. i. (1903), pp. 336–7.

10   Appendix A.

11   Necessarily approximate—see H. C. Darby, *The Domesday Geography of Eastern England*, (Cambridge, 1952), p. 212.

12   Waltham (Abbey) (40 hides), Barking (30), Southminster (30), Aedulvesnasa (the Sokens) (27), Littlebury (25), Tillingham (20, 6 acres), Clacton (20), Walden (19½), Debden (16½) and Clavering (15). For a consideration of the reduction of the Writtle hidage between 1066 (16 hides) and 1086 (14 hides), see p. 5.

13   *Barking:* T.R.E., 100 *villani*, 50 *bordarii*, 10 *servi* ; 1086, 140 *villani*, 90 *bordarii*, 6 *servi* (D.B., ii, f. 17b).

Walden at £50 (£36) and the others mentioned all at appreciably smaller amounts. While the absolute significance of any of these figures is unknown, relatively they show something of the importance of Writtle in relation to the County as a whole.

Whether it was a place of administrative importance for the County or indeed for the Hundred of Chelmsford in which it lay before or immediately after the Conquest cannot with certainty be established. It would not be unreasonable to conjecture that as the sole royal manor in the Hundred it would have been the place where royal decisions affecting not only Writtle but all the surrounding communities would be made known. As the figures set out in Appendix B and summarised on the map[14] show, only Great Waltham, parcel of the great possessions in Essex of Geoffrey de Mandeville, had a recorded population in any degree approaching that of Writtle. Chelmsford, which gave its name to the Hundred and where presumably the Hundred met,[15] was among the very smallest of the communities; it had indeed suffered a reduction in its tiny population between 1066 and 1086[16] and was but poorly linked by roads with the rest of the County.[17] Moreover, there is some documentary support for conjecture. The Hundred Rolls describe the meeting place of the ancient sheriff's county court as being 'a green place in the Chelmsford Hundred'. Although the Rolls date from the 13th century, it is most unlikely that such a meeting place determined by ancient and inviolable custom, had been altered since Saxon times, even if there were in fact more than one point of assembly.[18] The description 'a green place' immediately suggests Writtle and in particular Greenbury,[19]

[14] Map I.
[15] Chelmsford is not the only hundredal division in Essex to take its name from a fording-place at which there was no settlement in 1086. Uttlesford in the north-west corner of the County derives its name from the fording-place close to the confluence of the river Cam with a tributary in the parish of Wendens Ambo. Unlike Chelmsford it was never to give its name to a parish. Just as the rivers Chelmer and Can created a division of the Hundred into North and South Chelmsford, so the Cam divided Uttlesford into East and West. See Reaney, *op.cit.,* pp. 233, 516.
[16] *Chelmsford*: T.R.E., 5 *villani*: 1086, 4 *villani*.
[17] See also p. 14 below.
[18] H. M. Cam, *The Hundred and the Hundred Rolls* (1930), p. 107.
[19] See p. 11 below and Map II. Miss Cam (*op.cit.,* p. 107) indeed states that evidence other than that of the Hundred Rolls shows that the county met at Writtle and also at a place called 'Langethorn' (probably Stratford Langthorne in the parish of West Ham), though curiously she appears to associate 'the green place' more readily with the latter.

upon which the View of Frankpledge and Court Leet were reputedly held on Whit Monday down to the 18th century.[20]   Yet firmer evidence for the administrative importance of Writtle is contained in a writ of William II which must be assigned to a date July 1099–1100.[21]   By it Suene of Essex was commanded that the lands, men and all things of Maurice Bishop of London should be quit of wardpenny, pleas and all other matters, as was proved at 'Writele' before the king's justices, among whom was Suene, by the Bishop's charters and writs.

Relating the Domesday statistics for Writtle to that manor alone without reference to the rest of the County, what kind of community emerges, if in shadowy form?   Although the hidage at which the manor was rated before the Conquest (16 hides) is large this wholly fiscal assessment bore no relationship to its actual extent.[22]   An area of 1,920 acres for the manor alone, or 2,310 acres if the lands of the sokemen and priest are included,[23] is impossibly low when related to the extent implicit in the perambulation of 1358,[24] in which the bounds appear to coincide with those of the Tithe maps of Writtle, 1843, and Roxwell, 1842,[25] or the 1st edition of the 6-inch Ordnance Survey, 1881.   The Ordnance Survey gives a combined acreage for Writtle and Roxwell of 13,568 acres.   That the Writtle of Norman times included Roxwell (not mentioned by name in the Survey) is evidenced by *Newlanda,* the manor of Count Eustace of Boulogne, which lay

[20]   Morant, *History of Essex,* vol. ii, p. 61. Strangely, in none of the extensive manorial records is the meeting place of the manor courts mentioned.

[21]   The writ survives only as a transcript in *Liber A siue Pilosus* (St. Paul's MS. W.D.I) and the *Rotulus Libertatum Ecclesie Sancti Pauli* (St. Paul's MS. A.69), printed in *Early Charters of St. Paul's Cathedral,* ed. Marion Gibbs (Camden Third Series vol. lviii, 1939), p. 17.

[22]   The method of assessing hidage first on the county and then by successive distributions upon the hundreds and vills inevitably meant a considerable discrepancy between the amount assessed and reality from the start. See J. H. Round, *Feudal England,* pp. 49, 63, 91; also F. M. Stenton's Preface to C. W. Foster and T. Langley *The Lincolnshire Domesday and the Lindsey Survey.*

[23]   While a hide of 120 acres seems to have been usual throughout the County, an extent of the Manor of Thorpe within the Soken, 1297 (E.R.O., D/DHw M1), indicates that it was not universal. Much of the land in the occupation of the tenants of this manor was still hidated at that date, with the rents and services laid upon the hide and not upon the individual holdings. A specific note in the extent states *Memorand(um) q(uo)d hyda in hoc manerio continet vij acras terre.*

[24]   E.R.O., D/DP M544 (16th-century copy).

[25]   E.R.O., D/CT 414, 301.

in the northern part of the modern parish of Roxwell.[26] Despite
the discrepancy in the figures for *Newlanda* given in the main
entry in Domesday and separately under the fee of Count Eustace,
there can be little doubt that the acquisition of that manor by the
Count after its annexation by Ingelric accounts for the drop in
the number of hides at which the manor of Writtle was assessed
from 16 to 14.[27] The assessment of 3 hides for *Newlanda* under
the fee of the Count could well be a scribal error, while it is perhaps
not without significance of further error that the due of £12 from
it given in the main entry equals the product of its value in 1066
(£5) and its value in 1086 (£7) in the other entry.

To the undoubted fact that Writtle included Roxwell may be
added the suggestion that at some time prior to the Conquest the
terra regis had comprised a yet greater area, taking in much, if not
all, of the later parishes of Chignal Smealy and Chignal St James
which are represented in Domesday by no less than six small or
very small estates.[28] This is suggested by the one large and two
small detached parts of the parish and manor of Writtle to be seen
both on the Tithe map and the 1st edition of the 6-inch Ordnance
Survey.[29] For it would seem the most likely explanation that
these became detached as a result of grants which divorced the
land dividing them from the manor and from its jurisdiction.

Examining the figures relating to the population of Writtle
again, one is not only struck by the comparatively large number
of tenants, touched on above, but also by the lack of freemen and
the evidence of social depression of the *villani* between 1066 and
1086, as on so many other Essex manors.[30] It will be observed
that the decline in the number of *villani* corresponds exactly with
the increase of *bordarii*. The attachment of significance to this
correlation must be tempered by the recognition that the decrease
in the number of *servi* may be accounted for by the assimilation
of some or all of them into the bordar class.[31] Against the

---

[26] The earliest known reference to Roxwell is in the *Taxatio Ecclesiastica* of 1291.
P. H. Reaney, *op.cit.*, p. 264. Ecclesiastically it remained a chapelry annexed to
Writtle until 1851.
[27] See Appendix A.
[28] See Appendix B.
[29] Shown on Map II.
[30] See p. 2 above and Appendix B.
[31] On some Essex manors there was a correlation between the figures for *bordarii* and
servi. See *V.C.H., Essex*, vol. i, p. 362.

general trend in Essex there was at Writtle a slight overall decline in population.

The close relationship between the number of demesne plough-teams and the number of *servi* to which J. H. Round drew attention[32] is well illustrated by the Writtle figures which maintain the proportion of 2 to 1 in the decline from 24 to 18 *servi* and 12 to 9 ploughs.   It will also be noticed that the same proportion obtained on the Bishop of Hereford's estate (2 *servi* to 1 plough), but not on that of Count Eustace (2 *servi* to 2 ploughs).[33]   There would also seem to be a relationship, though not so precise, between the decline in the number of *villani* (24.74 p.c.) and the number of ploughs of the men (29.69 p.c.).

From this consideration of population and plough teams arises the inevitable question which has taxed the ingenuity of even the best interpreters of the Domesday Survey: if there was a reduction in the numbers of tenants and ploughs between 1066 and 1086, what did this signify for the economy of the manor?   While on most manors there is a yardstick of annual values at the two dates, this is not the case with Writtle, for it is impossible to say whether the render of 10 nights' 'feorm' and £10 in 1066 represented more or less the £100 of 1086.   Even so, as is known from other cases, a reduction in the number of ploughs does not necessarily bring about a diminution in value.[34]   It would seem unlikely that the value of 1086 represented a smaller annual value.   A possible explanation of the smaller number of ploughs would be a change in the pattern of farming, say, to an increase in the number of sheep pastured, but there is no evidence to support this, for the livestock figures show no variation.[35]   If there was no reduction in the amount of arable cultivated, as the statistics for woodland

---

[32] *Ibid.,* pp. 361–2.

[33] See Appendix A.

[34] The value of the manor of Thaxted, for instance, rose from £30 to £50, despite a slight decline in population and a sharp decline in the number of ploughs (which, the Survey states specifically and unusually, could be increased to restore it to the figure from 1066).   An increase in the number of beehives from 10 to 16 and of mills from 1 to 2 can only account for a part of the increase in value.   Moreover, an Englishman had been found who was willing to pay £10 above the value of £50 for the lease. D.B. ii, f. 38b.

[35] It may be pondered, of course, how the figures for 1066 could have been known so accurately twenty years later or allowing for the variable incidence of murrain how such a coincidence of figures could have occurred.

may suggest, then it can be surmised that by more onerous services the smaller number of ploughs in 1086 was coping with the same (? even greater) acreage.

Whether there was a greater area for cultivation in 1086 is a question raised by the details of woodland for swine. While the amounts of woodland on the estates of Count Eustace and the Bishop of Hereford remained static, there was a reduction of one fifth—from woodland for 1500 to woodland for 1200 swine. Whatever its significance in terms of acres, the figures for 1066 represent an extensive area of woodland and the reduction is proportionately considerable.[36]   It cannot be accounted for by an upsurge in demand for timber—the amount involved is too great. It is hardly likely—least of all on a royal manor—that the reduction represents wanton destruction.   One is thrown back, therefore, despite the smaller number of ploughs, to the conclusion 'that the loss of woodland represents that extension of the cultivated area (*terra lucrabilis*)that was always in progress'.[37]

There is some little evidence of assarting in Writtle in the first half of the next century. By an undated charter King Stephen granted in alms to Robert the monk, for the soul of himself, his uncle, King Henry and his wife Queen Matilda, the hermitage which Robert had made in 'my forest of Writela', as the enclosure and great ditch to the north secure, with everything necessary to provide his buildings, fire, pasture for his animals and his enclosure in the forest.[38]   When Henry II, with concurrent charter from Robert,[39] granted to the Abbey of St John the Baptist of Colchester the hermitage, by then known as *Bedemannesberga,* so that two monk priests dwelling there might always beseech the mercy of God for the salvation of the King and the souls of past kings, the Abbey was expressly granted *inter alia* immunity from assarts, as well as from hambling dogs and pannage, and the right

---

[36] For an interesting discussion of this problem, including an account of a revival of the practice of keeping swine in Sussex woodland in this century, see G. H. Fowler, *Bedfordshire in 1086: An Analysis and Synthesis of Domesday Book* (Quarto Memoirs of the Bedfordshire Historical Record Society, vol. i, 1922), pp. 62–3.

[37] J. H. Round, *V.C.H., Essex,* vol. i, p. 378.

[38] *Cartularium Monasterii Sancti Johannis Baptiste de Colcestria* (1897), p. 52. The hermitage stood close to a wide track which is possibly the remains of a Roman road to Writtle. A fragment of the hermitage which still stands has Roman tile in its fabric (*Reports* of the Royal Commission on Historical Monuments, Essex, vol. ii).

[39] *Cartularium Monasterii Sancti Johannis Baptiste de Colcestria,* pp. 38–9.

to have their men collect nuts in the surrounding forest in due season.⁴⁰ A general confirmation by Richard I to the Abbey of its possessions is more specific, granting quittance of 24 acres of assart with all their liberties. The only other evidence of assarting which has been found stems from the early 13th century, in a charter relating to Montpeliers Farm.⁴¹ By it Walter de Broma granted to Sawal de Sutwode 'all the land which Roger the gardener (*garde-narius*) held of me and an acre of my assart in Bromwode which lies next the aforesaid land and three acres in the same assart which lie between the highway towards London and the land which Roger de Wolvestune holds of me in width and in width (*sic*) from the highway from Writele to the stream which comes from the well of Rochee . . .'

Both these examples, it will be noted, occur in the remotest corners of the manor, indicating perhaps that by the early years of the 13th century, clearance of woodland (other than that which it was desired deliberately to conserve) had reached the less good London Clay and Bagshot Beds of the highest ground and in central territory was at an end. The first example cannot be used to suggest that this may have been the case a century earlier, because of the special nature of the assart, i.e. appurtenant to a hermitage.

As the Domesday Survey throws no light on the true extent or location of clearance by the Conquest, the evidence of place-names must be relied upon to fill some of the gap. Looking at the Ordnance Survey sheets or the Tithe maps and awards, a reasonably practiced eye will quickly realise that Writtle is one of those large Essex parishes with several scattered hamlets, each with a common or green, sometimes of considerable extent, whose names are indicative of islands of clearance in a sea of woodland or scrub.⁴² Very close to the principal settlement at Writtle was Oxney

---

⁴⁰ *Cartularium . . . Colcestria*, p. 45. A manuscript estate map, dated 1783 (E.R.O., D/DP P23), shows this assart in the far south-west corner of the manor surrounded on three sides by woodland and its fourth side abutting on waste; indeed, the current 1-inch O.S. sheet shows it similarly, though the waste has been enclosed. Its origin is still enshrined in the name of the farm, Monks and Barrows, a corruption of Monks at Barrow found as early as the late 15th century.

⁴¹ Preserved among the muniments of Wadham College, Oxford. Transcribed by C. R. Cheney in 'Medieval Charters relating to the Manor of Mountpillers, Writtle Essex', p. 2. Typescript, copy in E.R.O. (T/A 139).

⁴² See Map II.

(Green), the enclosure for oxen;[43] about two miles to the south-west lay Edney Common, the enclosure of Eada or of Eadluin or his people. Here, no doubt, the names enshrine some of the earliest efforts by the Saxon settlers to tame the woodland and scrub. Radley Green and Newney Green may well be pre-Conquest in origin also, but in the case of Highwood Common, Cooksmill Green and Loves Green the names give no clue whether or not they became hamlet settlements in Saxon times.[44]

It will be noticed on Map II that all these hamlets with their greens or commons are located in the central and southern part of the manor, with none further north than the Roxwell boundary with Writtle. The impression is that the Roxwell area was generally less wooded, on the evidence of place-names. Tye Hall, later found as a submanor, may represent a 'lost' area of common pasture[45] in the central part of Roxwell; and the field-name Rid(d)en is also found in Roxwell from the late 14th century.[46] Whether this derives from *ryden* (cleared land) or *hryding* (clearing), it is indicative that the area was by no means without woodland. There is little place-name evidence of early settlement in Roxwell. Armswick Farm may derive from 'the dairy-farm of the Earningas'[47] and Boyton Hall may also be an ancient site. In the case of the former, it will be observed that this too is on the Writtle-Roxwell boundary and the latter close to the river. The estate of Count Eustace in Roxwell called *Newlanda* was in existence before the Conquest, but its name is no doubt evidence of its comparatively late creation.

Thus the Domesday Survey, place-names, the Ordnance Survey, the visual evidence from field-work, all point to Writtle having still in the 11th century a very considerable area of woodland. But only later documentary evidence reveals that the whole manor was regarded as an outlier of the royal forest of Essex which covered

---

[43] -(h)ey from O.E. (ge)haeg, an enclosure. See P. H. Reaney *P-N.E.*, p. 282.

[44] *P-N.E.*, pp. 278, 264, 280, 281, 282. The earliest reference to Highwood occurs in 1274 in its Latin form *Alto Bosco*. Cooksmill is to be associated with the Cook family. A mill was built there by Richard Cocus in 1274. Loves Green is to be associated with the family of Robert Love (*fl.c.*1306).

[45] Tye derives from OE.*teag* and appears at first to have had the meaning, in Essex where it is widespread, of an outlying common and then later to have been applied to enclosures, particularly in areas of old woodland, where *(ge)haeg* is also frequently found. See *P-N.E.*, p. 591.

[46] See, for example, E.R.O., D/DP M219.

[47] *P-N.E.*, p. 264.

much of the County. The Domesday Survey, indeed, makes no direct reference to the forest and only one oblique one, which is included under the main entry for Writtle.[48]   It is possible that despite the phrase *accepit de manerio,* the 'king's woods' of which the former swineherd became forester may have been those of Writtle.   It would be reasonable that Robert Gernon, who apparently already had the forestership of Essex by 1086,[49] should assign to him an area of forest with which as swineherd he would have been familiar.   Some strength is given to this by the fact that the office of forester of Writtle was appurtenant to a messuage and carucate of land in 1328.[50] This holding is identified as the submanor called Wallextons.[51]

Although Writtle was a non-nucleated village, there is no reason to doubt that the principal—and perhaps first—settlement was as today about the triangular green which from the 13th century is found recorded as Greenbury.[52]   When the first Saxon settler came to that immediate area, it had much to commend it: less wooded than the surrounding terrain, with good pasturage along the banks of the river Wid and the river Can which meet a little more than half a mile north-east of the green. Greenbury stands on a patch of gravel resting upon the boulder clay which covers much of the manor and extending from the river Wid westwards to almost the far limits of Oxney Green. Apart from the nearby river, a small stream[53] traverses the area to supply its several ponds. Moreover the water level provides an abundant supply for wells at no great depth at many points.[54]   With nearby Oxney Green[55] the triangular area of Greenbury may well have been in

---

[48]   D.B. ii, f. 5b. And in Harold's time there was 1 swineherd rendering the customary due to the manor and seated *(sedens)* on 1 virgate of land and 15 acres; but Robert Gernon *(grino),* after the king came (into) England took him from the manor and made him (a) forester of the king's woods *(silva).*

[49]   *V.C.H., Essex,* vol. i, p. 347.

[50]   Extent of Manor of Writtle, 1328 (E.R.O., D/DP M540).

[51]   In 1242 Roger de Wollaston was forester. See *Select Pleas of the Forest* (Selden Society, vol. xiii, 1899), pp. 73–4.

[52]   See Map II.

[53]   Referred to in records as the 'leete' (O.E. *(waeter)-(ge)laet,* a watercourse). Preserved today as a name in the Leete Hotel close to the green.

[54]   J. C. Thresh, *Report on the Water Supply to the Village of Writtle in the Chelmsford Rural Sanitary District,* N.D. (c.1890).

[55]   See p. 8.

effect pounds for the protection of the cattle from human and animal marauders. The layout of the village seen on later maps indicates a degree of defence in depth about the green. The defensive element is also demonstrated by the fact that in 14th and 15th century records the area of Greenbury is called *infra barras*,[56] showing that there was some physical enclosure of the area.

From the early 13th century it is known that the manorhouse was situated not at Greenbury but about a quarter of a mile away to the north. This is at variance with the interpretation of Greenbury as 'the manorhouse by the green',[57] but when the documentary evidence is married to the results of archaeological investigation, there are very strong reasons for believing that the manorhouse was moved to its more distant site in about 1211. This is the year given by Stow in his *Annals*[58] when 'the king's house at Writtle was builded', without citing any authority. The Pipe Roll for that year, however, does record the expenditure of 20 marks upon the work of the King's houses at Writtle.[59] This could refer to the repair and renovation of existing buildings, but an excavation of the site in 1957 under expert direction found no evidence of a layout earlier than the first half of the 13th century. The only signs of earlier occupation were of a small Iron Age settlement.[60] It is likely, therefore, that the manorhouse before 1211 was indeed 'by the green'.

To suggest where its exact site may have been is to speculate, for there is no direct evidence. A three-acre croft called Oldbury just to the west of the northern tip of Greenbury[61] is suggestive, but there is nothing further to support the place-name evidence. It was not part of the demesne or if it had been it had ceased to be so by

---

[56] See, for example, E.R.O., D/DP M232.

[57] *P-N.E.*, p. 273.

[58] Howe's edition (1631), p. 168.

[59] *Pipe Roll, 13 John* (Pipe Roll Society, N.S. 28, 1951–2), p. 113.

[60] P. A. Rahtz, *Excavations at King John's Hunting Lodge, Writtle, Essex, 1955–57* (Society for Medieval Archaeology Monograph Series: No. 3, 1969). The manorhouse, popularly known as King John's Hunting Lodge in modern times, was in a decayed state by 1521 (See Survey of the Duke of Buckingham's lands after his execution in 1521, P.R.O. E36/150, pp. 68–9) and largely demolished or a ruin by 1566 (see Survey, D/DP M1325).

[61] For description of the croft and its abuttals, see Survey, 1564 (D/DP M548, p. 141).

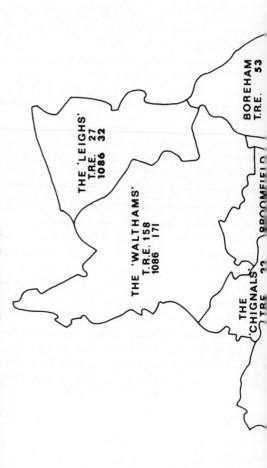

MAP 1

DOMESDAY POPULATION
Chelmsford Hundred

THE 'LEIGHS'
T.R.E. 27
1086 32

THE 'WALTHAMS'
T.R.E. 158
1086 171

THE
'CHIGNALS'
T.R.E. 22

BROOMFIELD

BOREHAM
T.R.E. 53

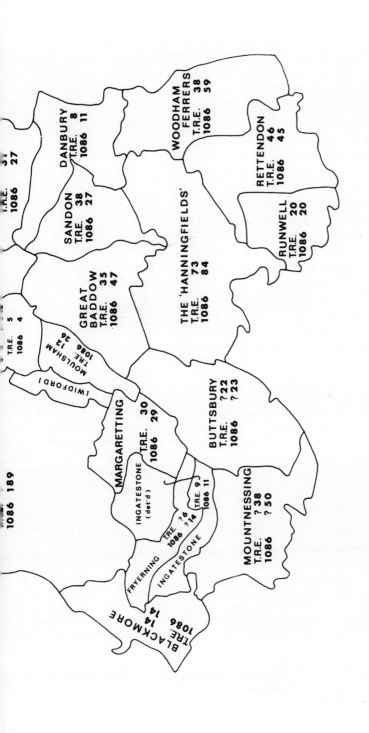

DANBURY
T.R.E. 8
1086 11

WOODHAM
FERRERS
T.R.E. 38
1086 59

RETTENDON
T.R.E. 46
1086 45

T.R.E. ?1
1086 27

SANDON
T.R.E. 38
1086 27

RUNWELL
T.R.E. 20
1086 20

THE 'HANNINGFIELDS'
T.R.E. 73
1086 84

GREAT
BADDOW
T.R.E. 35
1086 47

T.R.E. 5
1086 4

MOULSHAM
T.R.E. 12
1086 26

[WIDFORD]

BUTTSBURY
T.R.E. ?22
1086 ?23

MARGARETTING
T.R.E. 30
1086 29

1086 189

INGATESTONE
(det'd)

FRYERNING
T.R.E. ?6
1086 ?14

INGATESTONE

T.R.E. 9
1086 11

MOUNTNESSING
T.R.E. ?38
1086 ?50

BLACKMORE
T.R.E. 14
1086 14

the reign of Richard II.[62]   A possible answer lies in the grant of the church of Writtle by King John to the Hospital of the Holy Ghost in the Church of St Mary in Saxia in Rome in 1204, whereby the Hospital of Writtle was founded as a cell of Pope Innocent III's foundation for the English.[63]   The envoy of the Hospital was not put into possession of the church until 1218 when it became vacant.[64]   Was therefore the site of the manorhouse of Writtle removed so that the old building might serve as the home of the brethren of the Hospital?   The size of the site and its proximity to the church[65] lend some colour to the possibility.   Against, it may be argued that there would have been some specific mention in the grant by King John to the Hospital of the Holy Ghost in 1204. But there is no specific mention in the grant of the lands and tenants, rights and privileges which the Hospital of Writtle enjoyed and which the later manorial records show gave their estate the status of a capital manor, with its own View of Frankpledge and Court Leet as well as Court Baron, divorcing it entirely from the jurisdiction of the Manor of Writtle.[66]

The Domesday Survey offers no more evidence of a church building in Writtle in 1086 than of a manorhouse, though equally this cannot be taken as proof of its non-existence.   Churches were only listed when they possessed endowments which were a source of revenue to the Crown.[67]   Under the Bishop of Hereford's lands, however, it is recorded that of the 2 hides and 20 acres held by the bishop 1 hide was the church's (*in ecclesia*) in King Edward's time and that there was then as in 1086 a priest.[68]   Another priest, to whom Harold had given a hide of land, is also mentioned in the

---

[62]   E.R.O., D/DP M189.

[63]   Charter Roll, 5 John, mem. 9; *V.C.H., Essex,* vol. ii, p. 200.

[64]   *Calendar of Papal Letters,* vol. i, p. 58.

[65]   See Map II.

[66]   See court rolls of the Manor of Romans Fee in the possession of New College, Oxford (microfilm in E.R.O., T/A 126).   Frequent entries on the court rolls of the Manor of Writtle, 14th–15th century, are annotated in a later hand 'Romans Fee', because the misdemeanours, etc., recorded could not be resolved through lack of jurisdiction (D/DP M189 *et seq*).

[67]   *V.C.H., Essex,* vol. i, pp. 423–4.   There is no mention of churches at Holy Trinity, Colchester, Chickney, Greenstead-juxta-Ongar, Hadstock, Inworth, Little Bardfield and Sturmer, all of which are reputedly of Saxon origin (*Inventories* of Royal Commission on Historical Monuments, Essex, vols. i–iv, 1916–1923); and only at Chickney is a priest mentioned.

[68]   D.B. ii, f. 26, a repetition of part of the main Writtle entry on f. 5b.

main Writtle entry and this land too was in the bishop's hands in 1086. A place of worship may, therefore, be postulated from at least the time of King Edward the Confessor. It cannot be said with certainty that it was on the site of the present parish church, which has no architectural features earlier than c.1230,[69] though the irregular-sided figure shown by a ground plan of the chancel and its projection at an angle from the nave perhaps give grounds for suspecting a rebuilding on the foundations of an earlier building. By 1143 there is direct evidence of a church in the grant of it by King Stephen to the monks of Bermondsey.[70] The church had presumably come to the Crown upon the death of Robert Bishop of Hereford in 1095, together with the lands which he held in 1086. The *cum omnibus pertinentiis* recorded in the Bermondsey *Annales* may, therefore, represent those lands or at least that part which had been before the Conquest in *ecclesia.* When or how the monks of Bermondsey lost the church of Writtle is not recorded in these *Annales* or elsewhere, but by 1204, as has been seen above,[71] it was at the disposal of the Crown and by 1218 in the possession of the warden and brethren of the Hospital of Writtle. The lands of the Hospital probably represent, therefore, the lands—or part of them—held by the Bishop of Hereford in 1086.[72]

---

[69] *Reports* of R.C.H.M., Essex, vol. ii, pp. 271–5.

[70] *Annales Monasterii de Bermundeseia* (Rolls Series, 1886), p. 437. 'Et eodem anno (1143) dedit rex Stephanus monachis de Bermundeseye ecclesiam de Writel cum omnibus pertinentiis suis'.

[71] p. 12.

[72] In this chapter the use of the term *ancient demesne of the Crown* has been deliberately avoided in view of the researches of Professor R. S. Hoyt published in his *The Royal Demesne in English Constitutional History: 1066–1272* (Cornell University Press, for the American Historical Association, 1951). If in demolishing much of the longstanding theories advanced by Vinogradoff and Maitland on this subject, he appears not always to give due weight to the continuity of institutions from the Anglo-Saxon to the post-Conquest era, Professor Hoyt has convincingly demonstrated that the legal concept of *antiquum dominicum corone* developed after the Conquest, especially from the reign of Henry II onwards, when the Crown was seeking the ruthless exploitation of the royal demesne. In considering the tenurial structure of the Manor of Writtle (Chapter IV) as seen in documents of the 14th century it will be proper to refer to the manor as being ancient demesne.

II

WRITTLE AND THE RISE OF CHELMSFORD

T he relative importance of Writtle as an administrative centre in the 11th century suggested by the evidence offered in the previous chapter arose primarily from the physical advantages of its geographical position. Travellers from London making for northern parts of the county could avoid fording the river Wid at Widford and the river Can at Chelmsford by passing through Writtle, whose rivers and streams, even if unbridged, would have been less of a problem to negotiate.[1] It is significant that Widford remains unrecorded as a community until 1202 and no mention of a bridge there is to be found before 1285.[2] The area along the Can at its confluence with the Chelmer has always been subject to flooding[3] not only in winter but at all times of heavy rain and the absence of bridges at Chelmsford must have meant that any route over these rivers was not infrequently impassable.[4] Moreover, there is one categorical statement, admittedly without documentary support being cited, but not without authority, that before 1100 'London way . . . lay through Writtle'.[5] Such considerations would appear to be an assurance that Writtle was the most likely place to become the county town from which royal government and justice would be administered.

Yet when the earliest records of central government—the Curia Regis Rolls, Letters Patent, Letters Close, etc.—are examined it is Chelmsford, not Writtle, which is generally named in the writs as the place of meeting.[6] Thus it was at Chelmsford that the Curia Regis sat in 1199 when the Bishop of London was granted a market

---

[1] See Map III.

[2] Reaney, *Place-Names of Essex,* p. 275.

[3] An extensive flood relief scheme has recently been engineered to obviate this danger.

[4] It is to be noted that the Romans made their settlement of *Caesaromagus south* of the Can in the Moulsham area. No significant discovery of that era has been found in Chelmsford on the northern bank.

[5] See p. 16 below. For a summary of the evidence supporting the statement see Supplement, pp. 19–22 and Map III.

[6] The history of Chelmsford, with particular reference to the growth of its High Street, is the subject of an intensive, as yet unpublished, study by Miss H. E. P. Grieve, B.E.M. B.A., who has with customary generosity made available to me the results of her researches.

charter in his Manor of Bishops Hall there;[7] in 1218 the justices itinerant met there[8] as did a Forest Inquisition in 1219;[9] it was the meeting place of the justices appointed to assess and to collect the fifteenth in 1225.[10] With the holding of pleas of the Crown in 1227[11] and the existence of the King's prison by 1256[12] it may be said that Chelmsford was recognised implicitly as the county town and much later statutory recognition merely recorded a long established fact.[13]

Only once in the 13th century is Writtle found as the place of assembly for the County before the king's representatives. As a result of the serious problem of vagrant malefactors in Essex, the sheriff was commanded in 1237 to summon to Writtle on the Tuesday before Pentecost, before John son of Geoffrey, Amaric de Sancto Amando, the King's steward, and William de Gulwarth, earls, barons, knights, freemen and four men and the reeve from each vill, to provide from the counsel of all the county how the king's peace might be served there against the malefactors wandering through those parts and disturbing the King's peace.[14]

What change of circumstances, what surmounting of natural disadvantages occurred in the century after Domesday to make Chelmsford a more suitable centre than Writtle for the execution of royal government and justice in the County? Camden unequivocally gives the honour of having wrought this fundamental change to Maurice Bishop of London who numbered the

---

[7] E.R.O., D/DM T28 (certified copy made 1650).

[8] *Calendar of Patent Rolls*, vol. i, 1216–1225, p. 208; *Book of Fees*, Part I, 1198–1242, p. 244.

[9] *Ibid.*, p. 218.

[10] *C.P.R.*, vol. i, pp. 563, 565.

[11] *Book of Fees*, Part I, 1198–1242, p. 353.

[12] *Calendar of Close Rolls*, 1254–1256, p. 361. There was a gaol at Writtle in 1202, but this may have been only for forest offenders. (*Pipe Roll, 4 John*, Pipe Roll Society, N.S. 15, 1937, p. 268).

[13] Colchester was named as the meeting place of the Justices in 1202 and 1206 (*Curia Regis Rolls*, vol. ii, 1201–1203, p. 134; *Feet of Fines for Essex*, vol. i, p. 40), but in the first instance, at least, as the case involved Richard son of Gilbert of Colchester, it was no doubt held there because 'the burgesses have the right not to be impleaded outside their city'. In any event, at later date, it was by no means unknown for the Assizes and Quarter Sessions to be held at places other than Chelmsford, *e.g.* Brentwood. See typescript Calendar of Essex Assize Files, 1559–1714, and Calendar of Essex Quarter Sessions Rolls, 1555–1714, in the Essex Record Office.

[14] *Calendar of Close Rolls, 1234–1237*, p. 532.

Manor of Chelmsford *alias* Bishops Hall among his possessions of office. In Philemon Holland's translation of Camden's famous work,[15] it is related that Chelmsford 'beganne to flourish when Maurice, Bishop of London, built the Bridges heere in the Raigne of Henry the First and turned London way thither which lay before through Writtle'. Given that Camden had some documentary source now unknown for this positive statement, it places the bridging of the Can and Chelmer between the accession of Henry I in 1100 and the death of the Bishop in 1107.[16]

Certainly Maurice is the most likely of the Bishops of London in the 12th century to have built the bridges, for it was he who began the construction of the great medieval cathedral of St Paul and would therefore have had the necessary engineering skill at his disposal. During recent work on the Chelmsford flood relief scheme archaeological support for Camden's statement has come to light with the discovery of coursing of Norman date close by John Johnson's elegant 18th-century bridge which today spans the Can.

The economic consequences of the building of the bridges were naturally as beneficial to Chelmsford as they were ultimately detrimental to Writtle. Not only did it bring the inevitable concourse of people from all parts of the county at those times when the 'King's business' was being transacted at courts and enquiries, but also wayfarers daily making their way to Colchester and other parts of the north and east of the County. As a result of this and of the grant of a market in 1199[17] and of a fair two years later,[18] trade and commerce began gradually to flow into the town. By 1274 a corn market was in operation.[19]

How early Writtle enjoyed a market is unknown. Indeed, no mention of it had been found until five years[20] after the grant of Chelmsford's market rights. Domesday Book is silent on the

---

[15] *Britannia*, 1st English edition, 1610. Holland (1552–1637) was born and educated in Chelmsford.

[16] The first known reference to the bridge over the Can linking Chelmsford to Moulsham occurs in 1201. (*Pipe Roll, 3 John*, Pipe Roll Society, N.S. 14, p. 73).

[17] E.R.O., D/DM T28.

[18] *Ibid.*

[19] *Rotuli Hundredorum* (Records Commission, 1812), vol. i, p. 143.

[20] *Pipe Roll, 6 John* (Pipe Roll Society, N.S. 18, 1940), p. 7. There are no references in earlier Pipe Rolls, because the manor was at farm.

point, but in view of the relative importance of Writtle in the surrounding area and the closeness of date in the earliest reference, it is not unreasonable to assume that it was in existence before the grant to Chelmsford. If this is so, it is curious that the Crown, to which the lordship of Writtle belonged should have seen fit to allow a rival market so close, well within the distance stipulated by the lawyers at which a market might be set up from another without constituting a 'nuisance'.[21] The consideration in hand paid by the Bishop of London for the privilege outweighed, no doubt, the advantage of maintained or even enhanced income from Writtle market.[22]

Indeed, the inevitable, though not rapid, result for Writtle was decline and total eclipse of its market. The *compotus* of the manor rendered by the Sheriff of Essex and enrolled on the Pipe Roll for 1230,[23] records an income of 4 marks *de exitu fori ejusdem ville.* By 1304, the market was being farmed for 20 shillings yearly.[24] An extent of the manor made in 1328[25] shows an increase to 26s. 8d. but this includes income from the annual fair.[26] In 1361 and 1377, *compoti*[27] give the annual farm from the stalls and tolls, with a certain custom called 'Aletol', as only 6s. 8d. By 1419 the market had long since yielded nothing and the annual fair a derisory 4d.[28] The fair appears to have been held only after 1306, when Edward I willed 'that there shall be a fair yearly at my manor of Writtle . . . for eight days, on the eve and day of All Saints and the six following days' and commanded the sheriff 'to cause the fair to be publicly proclaimed throughout his bailiwick and to be held'.[29] If its creation was conceived as a

---

[21] Bracton, for example, defines the distance at 'six leagues and a half and the third part of a half' (De Legibus, f. 235b).

[22] The considerable increase in the number of places which were granted market charters at this time is dealt with by G. H. Tupling, 'Markets and Fairs in Medieval Lancashire', in *Essays in Honour of James Tait* (1935).

[23] *Pipe Roll, 14 Henry III*, (Pipe Roll Society, N.S. 4, 1927), p. 162.

[24] P.R.O., C.133/113 (1)

[25] E.R.O., D/DP M540.

[26] See below.

[27] D/DP M559, 560.

[28] Extent, D/DP M546. *Et erat ib(ide)m antiquo temp(or)e vnu(m) m(er)catu(m) quol(ibe)t die Lune quod modo non est tentu(m) ideo non extendit(ur).*

[29] *Calendar of Close Rolls*, 1302–1307, p. 408. By 1419 the fair was held only on one day a year, on the Feast of St. Leonard (D/DP M546).

means of replacing the declining income from the market it was singularly unsuccessful.

With its decline in importance, by-passed by travellers and those attending the courts of the county,[30] Writtle became an inward-looking community, jealous of interference by outside authorities and organs of justice, whether central or local, for the expression of which its rights and privileges provided the necessary apparatus.[31]

[30] An analysis of the numerous cases of assault presented at the annual court leet, for example, reveals very few involving strangers in the period 1378–1450 (D/DP M189–255).

[31] This aspect is developed in Chapter VII.

SUPPLEMENT TO CHAPTER II

'London Way ... Which lay Before Through Writtle'

T he support for this statement lies in the build-up of evidence from a variety of sources, which is expressed on Map III. The cartographical evidence gives two possible routes marked 'Way 1' and 'Way 2' on the map, both of which avoid any crossing of the river Wid, but other material favours heavily the first of these. The key document is the early 13th-century charter relating to Montpeliers Farm, among the muniments of Wadham College, referred to above.[1]   One of the parcels of land granted by it is described as *tres acras in eodem assarto que iacent inter cheminum regale versus London' et terram quam Rogerus de Weuleustune tenet de me in latitudine et in longitudine a chemino versus Writele usque ad rivulum qui venit de fonte de Rochee ...'* 'Rochee' is a lost place-name which has been found only in certain of the charters relating to Montpeliers Farm,[2] but they place it conclusively in Writtle adjacent to Southwood which covered the extreme southern area of Writtle and the large detached portion of the parish of Chelmsford. More specifically, they locate Montpeliers Farm *apud Southwode et la Rohey*.[3]   While the three acres in the assart cannot be precisely placed within the known area of the farm,[4] it must have abutted at some point on 'Way 1'

[1]   p. 8.
[2]   'Medieval Charters relating to the Manor of Mountpillers, Writtle, Essex', transcribed by C. R. Cheney, pp. 93, 120, 124–5, 127, 133, 135–6, 147. It appears variously as 'Rochee', '(la) Roc(h)ey', Rokhey'.
[3]   Cheney, *op.cit.,* p. 133. Quitclaim by Sawal de Hanygfeud to John Mompyler of 'Writele' of the actions and claims against the lands and tenements formerly of Adam de Suthwode, which John Mompyler holds in 'Writele' and 'Chelmesford' at 'Suthwode' and 'la Rohey', dated 10 January, 9 Edward II (1315/16). It is worthy of note that the three acres in the assart in the early 13th-century charter mentioned above were granted by Walter de Broma to Sawal de Sutwode, whom another charter, undated, but c.1250 (*op.cit.,* p. 7), shows to be father of Adam above. Sawal de Hanygfeud who made the quitclaim is described in another charter (*op.cit.,* p. 86) as the husband of Margery, daughter of Adam de Suthwode. This genealogical evidence tends to confirm further that the three acres in the assart are part of Montpeliers Farm.
[4]   The earliest map of Montpeliers Farm known is among the muniments of Wadham College and is dated 1729 (photograph in E.R.O., T/M 304). The area given is that plotted on Map III.

in proximity to one of the two streams also marked on Map III. The mention of the road (*chemino*) to Writtle as well as the high-way (*cheminum regale*) to London argues strongly for the more southerly of the two streams, having regard to its relationship to 'Way 3', though the rising of the northerly stream close to the farm is suggestive of the *rivulum qui venit de fonte de Rochee*. After the main way to London had been turned through Chelmsford, the postulated road from Writtle comes to be known as the way to Margaretting or to Ingatestone, both on the route to London ('Way 4').

It remains to attempt to identify the way a traveller having arrived at Writtle from London would have then taken to reach Chelmsford. If one looks at any map of the area, there are three possible routes ('Ways 5, 6 and 7'). There is no documentary support, however, for 'Way 5', which in 1328 is described merely as 'the road (*strata*) from the Manor gate unto the church where the ashes grow'[5] and in 1361 as 'the road from the Manor gate to the cross';[6] not until 1564 has it been found referred to as 'the highe waye from Wrytell to Chelmsford'.[7] It would appear likely that this way was first created or developed from a field path with the building of the manorhouse in about 1211.[8] Similarly, there is no evidence for 'Way 6', nor is it likely to have been a route before the building of the bridge over the Can at Chelmsford. 'Way 7' is today mostly a rough track known as Lawford Lane with the status of a bridle path, but at points where it is now overgrown by thicket or has not been encroached upon its carriage-width is still readily discernible.[9] It is referred to in court rolls of the medieval period as 'Lulfordstret', 'Lollefordstret' and 'regia via in Lollefordstret';[10] as late as 1739 it is referred to as 'the High road',[11] though there is no doubt that it had long since been little used by that date.[12] It is never called

---

[5] Extent, 1328 (D/DP M540).
[6] Compotus, 1360—1 (D/DP M559).
[7] Survey, 1564 (D/DP M548).
[8] See pp. 11—12.
[9] See illustrations opposite.
[10] Court rolls, 1423/4. 1452/3, 1467/8 (D/DP M228, 257, 269).
[11] Court book, 1736—1740 (D/DP M1455).
[12] Legal recognition of the disuse of Lawford Lane did not come until 1871, when it was reduced in status to a bridle path by the Enclosure Award of Writtle and Roxwell (E.R.O., Q/RDc 68).

LAWFORD LANE
The full width of the lane between the ditches along this
stretch is 18—20 feet.

LAWFORD LANE BRIDGE
Note the stumps of the piles indicating the width of the old
wooden bridge.

specifically in these references the highway from Writtle to Chelmsford. This would be unlikely, for by the date of the earliest the bridge over the Can had been in use possibly over two and a half centuries and the route through Moulsham found preferable because shorter.   There is a strong possibility, however, that a highway given as an abuttal in an inspeximus and confirmation of a charter of Robert de Brus, Lord of Annandale, made in 1292,[13] is identifiable with Lawford Lane. It described the bounds of a piece of pasture as the king's highway running from the market in Writtle to Chelmsford and the meadow late of Eustace de la Brome. By plotting the abuttals of holdings given in detailed surveys made in 1564 and 1594—5,[14] 'the olde market place' may be sited as shown on Map III; and the location of Eustace de la Brome's meadow somewhere between Lawford Lane and the rivers Wid or Can may perhaps be inferred by the proximity of Bromfelde, part of the demesne,[15] to the west of the way.

The balance of evidence is thus in favour of the way from Chelmsford to London lying (before the building of the bridges) along the route formed by 'Ways 8, 7 and 1' until it meets the reputed Roman road ('Way 4') at Margaretting, which leads to London by way of Ingatestone, Brentwood, Romford, Ilford and Stratford.

[13] *Calendar of Charter Rolls, 1257—1300*, vol. ii, p. 412.
[14] D/DP M548, 549.
[15] D/DP M548.

III

THE FIELDS, WOODS AND COMMONS OF WRITTLE

For reasons which will become apparent, it is appropriate to treat the demesne and tenants' land separately.

The Demesne Arable (See also Map IV).

The earliest direct reference to the demesne arable after Domesday occurs in 1304, in the *inquisition post mortem* of Robert le Brus senior,[1] in which the total acreage is given as 1200 acres *per minus centum acras.* An Extent of 1328,[2] which relates to the two third parts of the manor belonging to John de Bohun, Earl of Hereford and Essex, gives his holding as 889 acres *per perticam xviij pedum* while a further 380 are ascribed to Richard de Waleys and Alianora his wife who held the remaining third part at her death in 1331,[3] a total acreage broadly agreeing with that declared in 1304. The 1328 Extent also gives the names of the component fields and their acreages belonging to Bohun's share of the manor:—

Name of Field	Bohun Acreage
Thorncroft	196
Rotfeld	101
Bradefeld	66½
Barleycroft	9½
Great Okele	290
Little Okele	130
Alfaresfeld	96
	889

A bailiff's *compotus,* 1360–1,[4] when the manor was no longer divided, confirms that the acreages of Thorncroft, Rotfeld, Bradefeld and Alfaresfeld given represent the whole and not two thirds of their respective extents. As Great Okele and Little Okele were lying uncultivated in 1360 and Barleycroft is not mentioned in the *compotus,* there is no similar confirmation of their acreages, nor is it to be found in other records. Having regard to the very considerable size of Great Okele it would seem

---

[1]   P.R.O., C133/113(1).
[2]   E.R.O., D/DP M540.
[3]   D/DP T18.
[4]   D/DP M559.

likely that these three fields were in the same case. Moreover, the *compotus* makes mention of two other fields called Westhey containing 234 acres and Little Bradfield containing 9½ acres which are not mentioned in the Extent of 1328 and which in their entireties must have formed part of the 380 acres held by Richard de Waleys and his wife.[5]

The identification of these fields on a map may be taken forward through an Extent of 1419.[6] Although curiously (for the manor at this date was no longer in divided ownership) it gives only the acreages of the Bohun two thirds,[7] making no mention of the remaining third part, it does describe generally where most of the fields were located.

Name of Field	Location
Thorncroft	(i) *versus Chopenes ex parte de Boyton'*
	(ii) *iuxta magnum Okele*
Rotfeld	*ex parte de Writele*
Bradfeld	*ex parte predicta (Writele)*
Barlycroft	(not given)
Great Okele	*tam ex parte de Writele quam ex parte de Boyton'*
Little Okele	*ex parte de Writele*

Although imprecise their general locations do indicate that Thorncroft lay at Boyton in the hamlet of Roxwell and abutted on Great Okele which lay partly in Writtle and partly in Roxwell; and that Rotfeld, Bradefeld and Little Okele were wholly situated in Writtle. Only the small close Barlycroft remains unidentified. The *compotus* of 1360 establishes that Westhey was also at Boyton and other later records that Retherwick lay close to the Writtle—Chignal St James boundary.

To find the disposition of these fields more nearly, it is necessary to correlate the two detailed surveys made in 1564 and 1594–5,[8]

---

[5] The remaining 136 acres of their share in the demesne are not positively identifiable, but was probably represented in part by a demesne field called Retherwick not mentioned in the account of 1360 but referred to in later records.

[6] D/DP M546.

[7] *Et sunt ib(ide)m de t(er)ra d(omi)nicali arabili (et) sep(ar)ali p(er) partic(am) xviij pedum p(ro)ut patet per vet(er)es extent(es) duar(um) p(ar)ciu(m) eiusdem Manerij (et) eciam p(er) informac(i)o(n)em Will(elm)i Chalke Firmarij tocius Manerij (et)c'. . .*

[8] D/DP M548, 549.

a manuscript estate map of 1783[9] and the Tithe maps and awards of Writtle (1843) and Roxwell (1842).[10] By the time the earliest of these records was made the demesne arable had been to some degree, and by the date of the estate map extensively, subdivided into smaller enclosures. Among the names of these have fortunately survived some of the names or other identification of the larger fields out of which they were formed.

Thorncroft does not survive as a name, but a 30-acre field called Choppin Shotte at the north-west extremity of Boyton Hall lands in the two surveys, which appears as two fields, Upper and Middle Choppins, on the 1783 estate map, is suggestive of its location. This is indeed confirmed by the identification of the area of Great Okele below.

Great Okele may still more easily be placed, for it is known from the 1419 Extent that it abutted on Thorncroft and extended south-eastwards over the Roxwell boundary into Writtle. Its identification with much of the later Boyton Hall Farm (discounting meadow and pasture dealt with below), as shown on the 1783 estate map, and the north-west part of the demesnes on the Writtle side is confirmed by a 150-acre field yet called 'greate Okelye' in the surveys.[11]

Little Okele abutted immediately on the south-east of Great Okele and extended down to the Chelmsford-Roxwell road. By the date of the earlier survey, it too had been split into smaller enclosures, but its name was perpetuated in the largest of these as Okeleyes. Linked to Little Okele by the demesne meadow Writelfanne was Rotfeld. In the surveys it survives too as the name ('Rootefeilde') of the largest of the subdivisions created by that time, though the name does not appear on the 1783 estate map.

Bradefeld, Alfaresfeld and Westhey had not survived in name or extent by the date of the earlier survey (1564) but on the basis of relative acreage and the established position of the other fields they were probably located as shown on Map IV.

The demesne arable was thus a great compact block of nearly

[9] D/DP P35.
[10] D/CT 414, 301.
[11] By 1783 this field had been subdivided, but the name was perpetuated in two of the closes—Middle Oakley and Pond Oakley.

Location of places mentioned in Chapter 1.

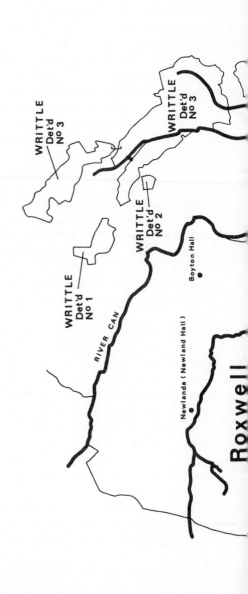

WRITTLE
Det'd
No 3

WRITTLE
Det'd
No 3

WRITTLE
Det'd
No 1

WRITTLE
Det'd
No 2

RIVER CAN

Newlands (Newland Hall)

Boyton Hall

Roxwell

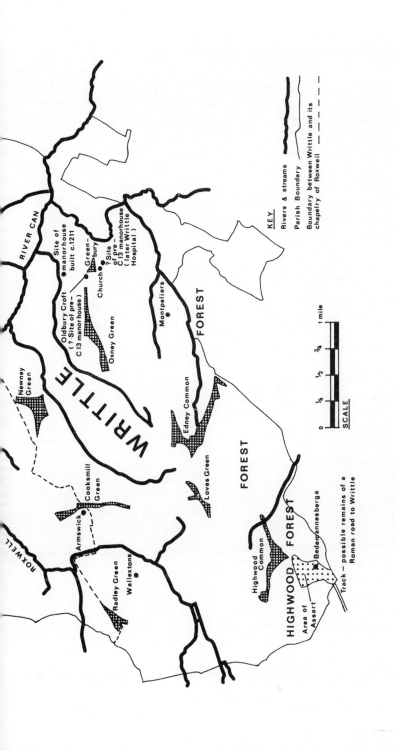

KEY

Rivers & streams

Parish Boundary

Boundary between Writtle and its
chapelry of Roxwell

RIVER CAN

Site of
manorhouse
built c.1211

Oldbury Croft
(?Site of pre-
C13 manorhouse)

Green-
bury

?Site
of pre-
C13 manorhouse
(later Writtle
Hospital)

Church

Oxney Green

Montpeliers

WRITTLE

Newney
Green

FOREST

Cooksmill
Green

Edney Common

Loves Green

Armswick

FOREST

Radley Green

Wallextons

Highwood
Common

HIGHWOOD FOREST

Bedenmannesberga

Area of
Assart

Track — possible remains of a
Roman road to Writtle

ROXWELL

SCALE

0   ¼   ½   ¾   1 mile

1,300 acres, generally to the north and north-west of the manor-house, riven only by the riverside meadows and pastures of the demesne and of other landholders.   In the period when the demesne was being farmed directly by the lord, the seven large fields and the small Barlycroft did not form the areal units of husbandry.   The 1328 Extent shows that a three-course rotation was practised in that period, whereby approximately one third of the arable grew winter-sown crops, another third Lent or spring-sown crops and the remaining third lay fallow.[12]   Each of these areas was called a *seisona* which might overlap from one field into the next or account for only a part of the total acreage of a field. Without indicating their utilisation the acreages of the 'seasons' belonging to the Bohun two thirds of the manor in 1328 were constituted as follows:—

First 'Season'		*Acreages*
In Thorncroft towards Chopynes		112
In Rotefeld		101
In Bradefeld		66½
In Barlycroft		9½
	Total	289

Second 'Season'		*Acreages*
In Great Okele		290
In Little Okele		30
	Total	320

Third 'Season'		*Acreages*
In Thorncroft on the part of Okele		84
In Little Okele on the part of Writtle		100
In Alfaresfeld		96
	Total	280

It will be seen by reference to Map IV that each 'season' was not a homogeneous area of arable, but was composed of separate blocks.   Thus the land of the first 'season' in Thorncroft was remote from the next block of that 'season' in Rotefeld; that in Bradefeld was separated from Rotefeld by the Great and Little

---

[12] For a more detailed discussion of the crops, see pp. 56–8.

Warren. It will also be noted that only Thorncroft and Little Okele contained areas of more than one 'season'.

The Demesne Meadows

The total acreage of demesne meadow was comparatively small and very largely in small parcels. The 1328 Extent details the two thirds in the hands of John de Bohun:—

Meadow	Acreage	
Boyton'fanne	5	
Wrytelefanne	11	
Hochemad'	3½	
Vechesmad'	2	
Longemad'	6½	
Holmad'	3½	
At the watermill in 'Pepyngho'		1 rood
Total	31	3 roods[13]

The total acreage was therefore something over 40 acres and, in so far as they can be located, the meadows have been plotted on Map IV. It is likely that they were all disposed along the two streams. All were several, except the 1 rood at the watermill in 'Pepyngho' *que iacet quol(ibe)t anno co(mmun)i post fenum leuat(um) (et) asportat(um) vsq(ue) f(estu)m Pur(ificacionis) beat(e) Marie virginis.* This is one of the very few references to common meadows and it would appear that by the early 14th century there was only the vestigial remains of a once more extensive area of such meadow.

The Demesne Pasture

As with the meadows the pastures were in comparatively small enclosures in which the acreages of the Bohun two thirds were:—

Pasture	Acreage
Greenacre	11
Little Warren	8
Great Warren with a piece of land called Vechesmor	15
In Rotefeld	14
Maria Apulton'	8
Total	56[14]

[13] There was apparently an increase in the acreage of meadow between 1304 and 1328, for the Extent of the *whole* manor made in the former year (P.R.O., C.133/113(1)) gives an acreage of 30.

[14] As with the meadows there was apparently an increase in the acreage of demesne pasture between 1304 and 1328, for the 1304 Extent records only 30 acres.

In so far as it is possible the pastures are plotted on Map IV. The parcel of 14 acres was apparently an area in the arable field called Rotefeld kept as permanent pasture; the pasture called Maria Apulton' was in effect an enclave in the same field.

This relatively small acreage of permanent pasture was considerably supplemented by the pasturage also available in the demesne arable fields. Every third year the whole of the fallow 'season' formed pasture for the lord's sheep; and around the peripheries of the fields under crops and elsewhere in them there was pasturage for other stock:—

	Acreage
In Thorncroft about the hedges and in a piece called 'Grenedych' '	8
In Rotefeld' about the hedges and in a slipe called 'Redfeldmad' '	4½
In Bradefeld' about the hedges	3
In Great Okele about the hedges and in the marl-pit there	5¾
In Thorncroft on the part of Okele about the hedges	3
In Little Okele on the part of Writtle about the hedges and in the marl-pit there	3½
In Alfaresfeld about the hedges	2
Total	29¾

The 1328 Extent also records an unspecified amount of pasture along the road from the manor gate to the church and the *compot* of 1360—1 and 1376—7[15] similar waste along 'Lollefordstrat'.

The Demesne Woodlands and Parks

In the contractions and expansions of the legal bounds of the royal Forest of Essex in the medieval period,[16] Writtle remained within the Forest because it was ancient demesne of the Crown.[17]

---

[15] D/DP M559, 560.

[16] See W. R. Fisher, *The Forest of Essex*, (1887).

[17] The perambulation of 1301, for example, declares that 'All the hundred of Chelmsford remains beyond the Forest except the vill of Writell which wholly remains in the Forest with its appendages, because it is ancient demesne of the lord King'. (Charter Misc. Roll No. 113, 27—29 Edw. I, translated by Fisher, *op.cit* pp. 393—9).

As noticed above,[18] the keepership of the Forest of Writtle was appurtenant to a messuage and carucate of land called Wallextons. A Forest Court held in 1250 took notice of a memorandum of the rights claimed by Isabel de Brus which makes mention of foresters, verderers and regarders for the half hundred of Chelmsford in the parts of 'Writtel' as well as woodwards of the constituent woods.[19]

While the whole of Writtle was legally forest, physically the main area of woodland, at least from the early 14th century and no doubt considerably earlier, was confined to the less good London Clay and Bagshot Beds of the higher ground in the south-west and south of the manor, and was reserved to the Crown in any leases of the estate made.[20] No doubt many of the visits of various monarchs recorded in the Patent Rolls and Close Rolls were associated with the chase. Not until after Isabel de Brus had received the manor in 1328,[21] as part of the exchange for her purparty of the earldom of Chester on the death of her brother John, is there evidence of the tenant having extensive rights in the woodlands. In 1243 the Regarders of the Forest in the Hundred of Chelmsford were commanded to make *nullum regardum . . . de boscis pertinentibus ad manerium de Writel' quod rex dedit Isabel de Bruis.*[22] Nevertheless, by the following year, the woods had been taken back into the king's hands, because it was alleged, that Isabel had committed waste. This, however, quickly brought a command to Richard de Munfichet, Steward of the Forest of Essex, to allow her to have the woods *secundum formam carte regis ei unde confecte.*[23] The confusion probably illustrates how unusual such a grant of forest in Writtle was.

As there is no record of any licence to enclose the principal park within the manor, it is likely that Writtle Park was created before the grant of the lordship to Isabel de Brus in 1238. The other park, Horsfrith, was enclosed by Richard de Brus following the

---

[18] See p. 10.

[19] Fisher, *op.cit.*, p. 18.

[20] For example, in the same year as he received a grant of the manor for life (1232), the Bishop of Chichester was commanded to let the Prior of Hatfield have 10 oaks in *forinseco bosco de Writel'* to help to repair his church and buildings which had been burnt down. (*Cal. of Patent Rolls, 1225–1232,* p. 483; *Cal. of Close Rolls, 1231–1234,* p. 53).

[21] *C.P.R., 1232–1247,* p. 224; *C.C.R., 1237–1242,* p. 59.

[22] *C.C.R., 1242–1247,* p. 92.

[23] *Ibid.,* p. 268.

grant of licence to impark his wood of Horsfrith which is within the metes of the forest of 'Writele' with his land thereto pertaining and to hold the same in fee simple.[24]

The 1328 Extent describes Writtle Park as having a circuit of 2½ leagues which corresponds approximately with the length of the boundary shown on the Tithe Map. The Surveys of 1564 and 1594–5 both give an acreage of 300 which corresponds nearly to that of the Tithe Award. Horsfrith Park is excluded from the 1328 Extent, as it belonged to the third part of the manor held by Richard and Alianora de Waleys. In the inquisition made on Alianora's death in 1331[25] only the value of its pasture and under-wood (£6) is given. Not until the dates of the two Elizabethan surveys do we find its acreage (260) stated.

The remaining woodlands not so imparked are not mentioned in any of the 14th-century extents (except 10 acres of wood called 'Horsleheg'' in Roxwell)[26] and there is no known estimate of their extent until the Elizabethan surveys. As neither a virtually unbroken series of court rolls from 1379[27] nor other sources yield evidence of any diminution of the wooded area since the 14th century the description of it in the surveys is probably applicable to the previous two centuries or more. The greatest sweep of woodland called Highwood ran in an arc of 270 acres along the south-west boundary of Writtle between the two parks; on the east of Writtle Park were the 120 acres of Great Edney Wood.

The Commons

The two great commons of the manor were in fact the woods of Highwood and Great Edney mentioned above. In the two Elizabethan surveys the former is described as 'one greate wood or com(m)on of pasture' and the latter as 'Greate Edney woode al(ia)s Great Edney Com(m)on'. In these 390 acres of woodland the tenants of the manor had rights of pannage and pasture, and avesage lists in respect of the former are frequently annexed to the court rolls.

While the earliest extent of these two commons is given in the

---

[24] *C.P.R., 1225–1232*, p. 304.
[25] D/DP T18.
[26] The similarity of the names 'Horsfrith' and 'Horsleheg' has led to some confusion in the past. References to the latter have been taken to refer to the former.
[27] D/DP M189 *et seq.*

surveys, there is no evidence that they had contracted much since the latter part of the 14th century, for the court rolls offer instances only of occasional grants of small parcels upon them. Indeed the economic climate was against any extension of large-scale enclosure[28] and the value of the commons as pasturage too high.

Further pasturage was provided by Little Edney Green (10 acres), Loves Green (3 acres), Cooksmill Green (30 acres), Radwell Green (20 acres), Newney Green (20 acres) and Great and Little Oxney Greens (20 acres) and Greenbury (3 acres). While analysis of the avesage lists shows that the two great woodland commons provided pannage for tenants over the whole manor, the small greens were reserved to those who lived in their vicinity.[29]

The Tenants' Lands

While the arable of the demesne was divided almost wholly into great fields, the general picture of the tenants' holdings given by surviving medieval charters and manorial records is one of small—often very small—enclosures; and this is applicable over the whole of the area of the manor and to tenements large and small. The piecemeal evidence of these documents is confirmed by the surveys of 1564 and 1594–5.[30]

Thus the 270 acres of Shakestons Farm in the extreme south-east and the 227 acres of Mountneys Farm in Roxwell were disposed respectively over 27 and 15 crofts;[31] the 24 acres of a tenement called Gorrells in the Highwood area and the 100 acres of Beaumont Otes in the large detached part of the manor to the north were contained in 5 crofts and 10 crofts and 2 meadows; a tenement called Puttpoles *alias* Lightfootes in the extreme west had 8 crofts totalling a mere 26 acres.

This overall uniformity, however, did not apparently arise from a common origin. For a thorough analysis of the two Elizabethan surveys related to the earlier records indicates the presence of a common-field system in the northern half of the manor, in

---

[28] See Chapter VI.
[29] 'Lyttle Edney grene beinge a Com(m)on of pasture to this hamlett . . .' 'There belongeth to this hamlet A com(m)on of pasture called by the name of Cookesmyll grene . . .' (Survey, 1595, D/DP M549).
[30] There is no evidence at all of any fundamental change in the field pattern in the period for which there is written record.
[31] Shakestons and Mountneys ranked as submanors. See Chapter IV and Map V.

Roxwell, which by the date of the earliest written evidence was
represented only by vestigial remains. Of the three so-called
common fields of which there is record, one lay within the Manor
of Newland Hall or Fee,[32] the second in the Manor of Newarks,[33]
and the third in the Manor of Writtle itself.[34] The field belonging
to Newland Fee is represented in the 1564 survey as 'xvj acr(es) in
the com(m)on feilde called Newland Fee' and abutted on all sides
upon enclosures, not described as being or having been part of the
common field. These 16 acres were in the tenure of one person
and formed part of Youngs Farm which was principally in the
Manor of Writtle. The common field of Newarks contained
approximately 45 acres, of which 5 were in the hands of a
manorial tenant (again the farmer at Youngs), the remainder was
demesne.[35] A map of Newarks made in 1620[36] shows that by
that date the five acres had been merged into the demesne, which
is confirmed by its absence from a map of Youngs Farm dated
1682.[37] The fragment of common field within the Manor of
Writtle totalled only 9 acres, divided into two parcels of 3 and
6 acres, of which the former belonged to a tenement called Suttells
and the latter to Fetches (later Thatchers Farm).[38] Exhaustive
analysis of surviving court rolls of the Manor of Newland Fee,
1448–1606,[39] court rolls, 1527–1649, and rentals, 1441–1768,
of the Manor of Newarks[40] and of Writtle, 1379–1553,[41] reveals
no extension of the acreages given in the two surveys, either by
way of description of parcels in records of transfers between
tenants and inheritances or in pleas between tenants or presentments for trespass.

---

[32] See pp. 4–5 above.
[33] The Manor of Newarks was very largely in Good Easter, but had a small enclave in
Roxwell, of which the common field was part.
[34] For their location, see Map IV.
[35] The surveys of 1564 and 1594–5 erroneously place the field in the Manor of
Newland Fee, but this is corrected by marginal notes probably added shortly after the
date of the later survey.
[36] D/DSp P1.
[37] T/M 280 (photograph).
[38] These 9 acres, alone of the fragments, are still called 'Common Field' at the date of
the Tithe Award of Roxwell, 1842, by which date both pieces formed part of
Thatchers Farm.
[39] D/DU 497/28–9.
[40] D/DSp M1–4, 19–30.
[41] D/DP M189–322.

In the northern part of the manor in the 14th to 16th centuries one finds then a situation similar to that found by Miss Levett on the manors of the Abbey of St Albans, where she too found the demesne arable divided into three 'seasons' for the purpose of crop-rotation, but with no sign of any like arrangement of the tenants' lands.[42] She was compelled on the evidence available to conclude that on the manors the three-field system[43] was either imperfectly developed or in decay. In the case of Writtle one can be, if hesitantly, more positive, for the extent of the great demesne fields and the proximity of the remnants of the three 'common fields' are very suggestive that there was an advanced state of decay; that in some great unrecorded redistribution of the lands of lord and tenants, the former's were consolidated into the large fields, the latter's into the small enclosures found in the extant evidence.

It is possible that the lord took over the original common fields, except those parts belonging to the other two manors, the tenants being compensated by assarts elsewhere. This accords certainly with the contrasting size of the demesne fields and tenants' enclosures. It accords also with the proposition based on place-name evidence that the northern half of the manor was the area of earliest settlement.[44]

The need for the redistribution of the lands of a community at some point, with the growth of population and the expansion of the area tilled, where cultivation of strips in the fields was the prevailing method, has been a logical step in the argument of recent study of the common-field system. Relying heavily so far on the researches of European scholars in their own countries, though there is some contributory evidence in England, the evolution of the system is viewed as a slow process, becoming fully developed only when the growth of the cultivated area and the need for greater efficiency demanded that the community as a whole co-operate to take over the regulation of the fields where previously

---

[42] A. E. Levett, *Studies in Manorial History* (Oxford, 1938), pp. 338–9.
[43] The use of the term 'three-field system' can be misleading, for on some manors at least the important element in the distribution of the lands among the 'seasons' was not the 'field' but the *quarentena*. See Dorothy Cromarty, *The Fields of Saffron Walden in 1400* (E.R.O. Publications, No. 43, 1966).
[44] See p. 9.

agreement between a few neighbours had sufficed.[45] The evolution of the field pattern in Writtle postulated above is not necessarily at variance with this theory up to the point in time where redistribution of the land among the cultivators became necessary; but it does indicate that at that point there was an alternative to the adoption of a more or less fully-fledged common-field system—farming in severalty.[46]

In the southern part of the manor no hint of common fields is to be found. The originally heavily wooded nature of the territory and its comparatively late clearance still taking place in the 13th century[47] no doubt militated against such a development. In this area of the manor it is sharing of the fields not by the community at large but by coparceners which is the characteristic in the documented period. It is a type of field-system consistent with a forested region, particularly as a later extension of the area of original clearance.[48]

Among the charters of the submanor of Montpeliers no less than 32 dating from the early 13th to the early 14th century relate to parcels of lands within crofts. Typical is an early 13th-century grant[49] from Albric de Sakeleston' to Sawal de Suthwod' of *duas acras terre in campo vocatur Hegefeld cum omnibus pertinenciis suis que iacent inter terram Galfridi fabri et terram Randulfi Bole . . . Preterea tres acras terre que iacent in campo qui vocatur paruus Sahelst(on') et siquid plus illis tribus acris habeatur et iacent inter terram Galfridi de ponti quam tenet de me et campum qui vocatur Welfeld . . .* An even better illustration of the relationship

---

[45] See Joan Thirsk, 'The Common Fields', in *Past and Present,* No. 29 (1964), pp. 3–25, where this theory is advanced in view of the failure of the explanations of the common-field system advanced by H. L. Gray (*English Field Systems,* Cambridge, Mass., 1915) and C. S. and C. S. Orwin (*The Open Fields,* Oxford, 1938) to accommodate more recent evidence on the subject.

[46] An investigation of other so-called 'early enclosed' Essex parishes would perhaps yield similar evidence. Some obviously had a largely pastoral economy and never a system of co-operative farming by either parceners or the community as a whole; but there are others which had a mixed-farming economy like Writtle (*e.g.* Great Waltham, West Tilbury) and in which at a late date there were vestigial remains of fields cultivated in strips.

[47] See pp. 7–8.

[48] It is not, however, necessarily evidence of late clearance if Vinogradoff's interpretation of Ine's Laws (688–694) *c.*42 is correct, for he assumes without question that the ceorls who 'have common meadow or other shareland' refers to coparceners and not to the whole local community.

[49] T/A 139, p. 5.

of this type of field, shared by coparceners, to clearance of woodland is another 13th-century charter,[50] whereby Richard le
Fanwreite gave to his son *pro homagio et servicio et pro viginti
solidis mihi datis in gersummam vnam acram terre mee cum
pertinenciis suis in villa de Writell' que iacet in campo vocatur le
Reden*[51] *inter terram Philipi le Brun et terram Galfridi Almar et
extendit se a terra mea vsque ad terram Elye adgor.* The shares in
such fields no doubt originated often from co-operative assarting,
though no charter unfortunately records this. One early 13th-
century charter[52] does, however, suggest that on occasion the
grant of a share in a field might be made to secure a financial
return on individual effort. By it Walter de Broma gave to Sawal
de Sutwode *vnam acram assarti mei in Bromwode . . . et tres acras
in eodem assarto.* Division might also arise from partible inheritance or from a grant to a son by his father or as a result of a
marriage settlement. By a charter of *c.*1250 Elias Bissop granted
to his son Ralph *quatuor acras terre . . . scilicet totam illam
croftam cum sepibus et fossatis que vocatur Longecroft in que
continentur due acre . . . et vna acra iacet in campo meo qui
vocatur Brodfeld in longitudine inter terras meas vnde vnum capud
tangit campum meum que vocatur Madfeld et aliud capud regale
vicum. Et quarta acra iacet in campo meo qui vocatur Dwne.*[53]
By three other grants of about the same date[54] Elias also gave to
his son two further pieces, each of 2 acres, in 'Brodefeld' and two
additional pieces, of 1 acre and 2 acres respectively, in 'Dwne'
('La Dune' in one charter). By another charter of similar date[55]
he had made a grant of 2 acres in 'Brodefeld' to a Ralph de Wyke;
and one of the four grants to his son[56] indicates that Elias had
given to his son-in-law Alwred de Mora an unspecified amount of
land in 'La Dune' *in libero maritagio cum Roisia filia mea.*
    It is to be specially noted that while the croft in the first grant
is specifically said to be enclosed with hedges and ditches, no such
description of bounds is given for the parcels in 'Brodfeld' and

[50] T/A 139, p. 91.
[51] 'le Reden' signifies clearance of woodland.
[52] T/A 139, p. 2.
[53] *Ibid.*, p. 10.
[54] *Ibid.*, pp. 11–13.
[55] *Ibid.*, p. 9.
[56] *Ibid.*, p. 13.

Dwne'. It follows that it must have been most convenient if not absolutely necessary for there to have been some agreement among the coparceners about the cropping of such fields. Thus when Robert de Sakelston' leased to Bertram de Montepessolano from Michaelmas 1282 for a year *duas acras terre in campo qui vocatur Stanfeld . . .* and *quatuor acras terre . . . in campo meo qui vocatur Burfel,* the lessor stipulated that the two parcels had to be sown with wheat and oats.[57] It has not been possible to find any evidence whether co-operation between parceners extended to pasturing the stubble of their fields after harvest. If it were done at all it would probably have been only for the benefits of manuring, for with the great areas of common and waste available, the stubble of the arable could not have been vital; manuring, however, did become important with more intensive cropping and was most easily done by grazing stock on the fields.[58] Certainly in the 14th century the demesne arable was manured by both sheep and cows, though there was insufficient for all the land.[59]

Just how long fields in Writtle shared by coparceners endured it is impossible to say. Certainly by the date (1564) of the earlier of the two Elizabethan surveys they had wholly disappeared. The process by which this took place, however, may be discerned in two other charters among those of the submanor of Montpeliers. One of *c.*1250[60] grants *vnam acram terre mee . . . sicut metis et divisis includitur et iacet in quodam campo vocato le Netherecroft . . .*; the other dated 1355[61] grants *quatuor acras terre sicut sepibus et fossatis includuntur in quadam crofta vocata Chandelerscrofte . . .* Such enclosures within enclosures would seem to explain the complex of small fields particularly characteristic of the southern half of the manor.

---

[57] T/A 139, p. 56.
[58] That this was understood at least by the 13th century is proved by *Walter of Henley's Husbandry . . .* (ed. E. Lamond, London, 1890), pp. 18–23.
[59] *Compoti,* 1360–1, 1366–7 (D/DP M559, 560).
[60] T/A 139, p. 38.
[61] *Ibid.,* p. 194.

IV

THE TENURIAL STRUCTURE

Contrary to some earlier statements, the Manor of Writtle was not coterminous with the ancient parish (which included Roxwell). The Domesday manor of Newland Fee[1] was held in chief of the Crown and its surviving records show that it had its own view of frankpledge and court leet, appointing among its officers a constable. So too, the Manor of the Rectory *alias* Romans Fee, which until 1391 belonged to the Hospital of Writtle and thereafter to New College, Oxford, had similar jurisdiction.[2] And, as has been seen in Chapter III, the Manor of Newarks intruded to a relatively small extent over the north-east boundary of the parish.

In so far as is possible, the lands of the manors are shown on Map V. By plotting the evidence of the extant records of these manors, manuscript estate maps and the Tithe Maps and Awards of Writtle and Roxwell,[3] it has been practicable to establish the areas of their demesnes and a considerable number of the tenants' holdings of the Manor of Newland Fee; but many of the tenants' holdings of the Manor of Romans Fee remain unidentified, particularly among the tenements about Greenbury. This problem was unresolved by the makers of the Surveys of 1564 and 1594–5, for they too were apparently unable to unravel the complexity of the holdings of that manor and other property belonging to the church which was quit of all rents to any manor. But it may be sufficiently seen by reference to Map V that much of the extreme north and west of the parish and a considerable number of islands of territory within its boundaries were excluded from the lordship of the Manor of Writtle. The Manor of Romans Fee had probably formed part of the *terra regis,* for it lacked copyhold tenure and at the view of frankpledge and court leet the common fine was not a fixed sum but was based upon ½d. from each decenner, as in the Manor of Writtle itself. The scattered nature of its territory is also

---

[1] See pp. 4–5 above.
[2] See p. 12 above.
[3] These records are described in the List of Original Sources Consulted at end.

characteristic of subinfeudation.[4]   What remains uncertain, is
whether it was first constituted a manor upon the endowment of
the Hospital in 1204 or is to be identified with the estate of the
Bishop of Hereford at the time of Domesday.[5]   The Manor of
Newland Fee, however, had at least two copyholds in Writtle[6] and
a certain common fine, suggesting that its creation before the
Conquest was not by way of subinfeudation, but by colonisation
and clearance of virgin land not formally part of the *terra regis*.

Apart from the fact that the Manor of Writtle itself was in the
hands of the Conqueror and the deduced evidence that it had been
part of the royal estates before the Conquest, there is nothing in
Domesday Book to suggest a tenurial structure different from that
on many other manors which were not and had not been in royal
hands. The absence of freeholders, the presence of sokemen, may
take on significance in the light of later evidence, but within the
context of the Great Survey alone it does not. For a further description of the classes of tenants and their holdings one must wait
until the early years of the 14th century. In the *inquisition post
mortem* of Robert the Bruce, senior, made in 1304,[7] mention is
made of an unspecified number of *liberi sokemanni* who paid
rents of assize totalling 36*li. 3s.*, *sokemanni tenentes* who held
17¼ virgates of land among them, *formanni* holding 7 virgates,
tenants of 10 virgates of *terre firmarie* and *sokemanni de Stana*.
The use of the terms *liberi sokemanni* and *sokemanni*, whatever
their precise significance, is an indication that here is indeed a
manor in ancient demesne.[8]   And when the court rolls of the
manor are turned to and the little writs of right close are found
stitched to the membranes and enrolled, this is doubly confirmed.[9]

---

[4] For another example, see my *Thaxted in the Fourteenth Century*, p. 7 and Map II
showing the location of the lands of the Manors of Horham Hall carved out of the
parent Manor of Thaxted.

[5] See pp. 12–13.

[6] Analysis of the court rolls and books has revealed 18 holdings, of which 14 were of
freehold tenure and 4 copyhold. One of the former and two of the latter were
situated in the adjoining parish of Margaret Roothing.

[7] P.R.O., C133/113(1).

[8] Pollock and Maitland, *The History of English Law* . . . (2nd. edn., 1923), p. 392, but
see p. 13, n. 72 above.

[9] For the significance of the little writ of right close, see Pollock and Maitland, *op.cit.*,
pp. 385–8. No example of the writ of *monstraverunt* has been found, but it was
probably used by the tenants of Writtle in their dispute with Robert the Bruce,
senior. See pp. 53–4.

The categorisation of the tenants in the inquisition dockets them so neatly and simply that one may suspect that it is misleading.

So it proves to be when the much more detailed Extent of two third parts of the manor, made in 1328, is analysed.[10] It is found that the misleading nature of the Inquisition lies in the fact that the same tenants are being classified both legally and economically, but no clue of this is given. In the Extent, the work *sokemanni* is entirely absent: instead, the tenants are classified as *liberi tenentes, maiores molmanni, minores molmanni, custumarii operarii, akermanni, foremanni* and tenants *ad voluntatem domini.* That the term *liberi sokemanni* in the Inquisition comprehends all these is proved by the fact that the gross rents of assize from them totalling 25*li*. 15*s*. 10½*d*. in the Extent is approximately two thirds of the 36*li*. 3*s*. said to be due from the *liberi sokemanni* in the Inquisition. The *liberi sokemanni* in the earlier document are not therefore separate from the *sokemanni, foremanni* and tenants of *terre firmarie* also listed in it but embrace them. On comparing the two documents more closely, the different terminology used in each may be equated thus:—

Inquisition	Extent
Some of the *liberi sokemanni* (a term also including the classes below)	*Liberi tenentes*
Sokemanni	*Maiores* and *Minores Molmanni* and *Custumarii Operarii*
Foremanni	*Foremanni* and *Akermanni*
Tenants *terre firmarie*	Tenants *ad voluntatem domini*

The legal definition in the Inquisition of *all* tenants as *liberi sokemanni* is, however, perfectly correct, being fully borne out by the later records. The Extent, on the other hand, misleads in describing one class as *liberi tenentes,* giving the impression that these landholders were no longer privileged villeins on ancient demesne, but had been enfeoffed of their lands which they held as freeholds at common law. This false impression is corrected when these

[10] D/DP M540.

MAP III

The Way from Chelmsford to London.

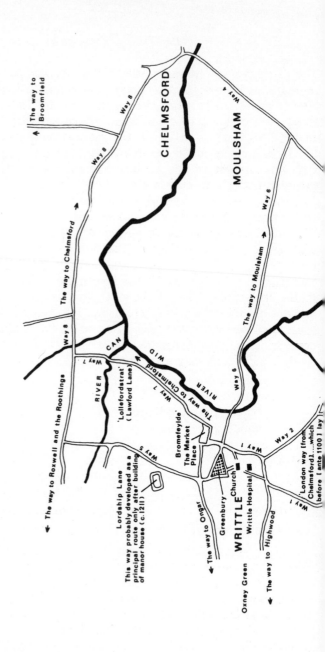

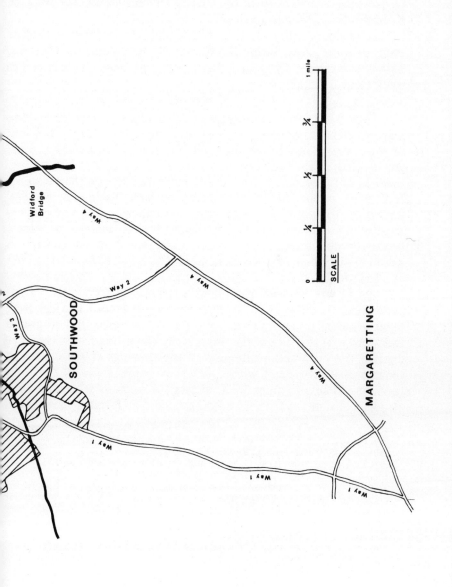

Widford
Bridge

Way 4

Way 2

Way 4

Way 3

SOUTHWOOD

Way 1

Way 1

Way 4

Way 1

MARGARETTING

SCALE

0   ¼   ½   ¾   1 mile

tenants are found availing themselves of the little writ of right close.[11] The absence of evidence on the court rolls that the writ was not available to all tenants or that some were precluded from transferring their holdings by charter underlines the accuracy of the definition in the Inquisition.

This overall equality of status in law had no economic equivalent even, in some cases, within the various classes of tenant. This may best be considered by an examination of each class, as described in the Extent of 1328.

Liberi Tenentes

As will be seen by reference to Appendix C,[12] the distinctive feature of these holdings was the prevalence of the virgate as a unit of size; even a number of those whose areas are expressed in acres are said to be parcels of virgates or fractions of virgates. This is, on the face of it, surprising, for with the universal use on the manor of feoffment as the means of transferring land, there was no legal inhibition to mobility[13] and one might therefore have expected greater fragmentation of the holdings. By this period the virgate is not normally found to any extent among the freeholds of manors not in ancient demesne, the tenants of which had the same freedom of alienation.[14]

If there was no legal disability for mobility, economic causes must next be sought. It is clear that while labour services were being exacted or even being 'sold' instead of formally commuted this was a brake upon the market in villein land.[15] This will explain the continuing integrity of the holdings of the classes of tenants in Writtle dealt with below, but not of those of the *liberi tenentes*. For as Appendix C shows no onerous labour services attached to any of their holdings; and a number were even

---

[11] For example, enrolments of Fines levied and Recoveries suffered in respect of the submanor of Wallextons, described in the Extent as a messuage and carucate of land held by a *liber tenens*, are to be found in the court rolls and books for 1561, 1659, 1740/1, 1783 and 1807 (D/DP M330, 403, 1459, 1462).

[12] The table accounts for only those holdings assigned to the two thirds of the manor held by John de Bohun. Owing to the disparity in rents for holdings of equal size, it represents approximately two thirds of the total value of rents from the *liberi tenentes* not two thirds of the number of holdings in their hands.

[13] This applies too to the holdings of the other classes of tenants.

[14] See, for example, the table of freeholds of the Manor of Thaxted in 1348 in my *Thaxted in the Fourteenth Century*, p. 10.

[15] *Op.cit.*, pp. 12–19, 23–26.

exonerated from such obligations as suit of court, relief, heriot and tallage (the arbitrary impost characteristic of ancient demesne).

The answer to this problem lies fortunately not in speculation but down the margin of the Extent of 1328. Against 23 of the 41 entries relating to the holdings of the *liberi tenentes* are written the words *p(er) cartam d(omi)ni Rob(er)ti de Brus, p(er) cart(am) R(oberti) de Bruys* and, in one case, *p(er) iij cart(as) R(oberti) de Bruys;* against two other entries *p(er) cart(am) Is(abelle) de Bruys* and a further entry has *p(er) cart(am) (?cart(as)) R(oberti) (et) Joh(ann)is de Bruys.* Thus the terms on which 27 of the 41 holdings were held of the lord of the manor rested on charters which had been issued within the previous 87 years. Those granted by Isàbel de Bruys may be dated between 1241, when she was given the manor in part exchange for her inheritance as co-heiress of the Earldom of Chester, and 1252, the year of her death. In the case of the charters ascribed to Robert de Brus, this may refer to Isabel's son, who held Writtle from 1252 to his death in 1295 or his son who was lord from 1295 to 1304,[16] when his son inherited; the last was deprived of his English estates upon his attainment of the Scottish throne in 1306.

One charter relating to a ½-virgate in the Extent, however, survives in a 16th-century copy and bears date Thursday in Pentecost Week, 26 Edward I (1298).[17] Also among the manuscripts at Wadham College, Oxford, relating to Montpeliers Farm, there are two original charters relating to holdings of the third part of the manor not contained in the Extent.[18] Neither is dated, but as 6 out of the 14 witnesses in the dated charter appear in one or other of them, they are fairly close to it in time, and this is, indeed, supported by the palaeographical evidence. As the dated charter, however, is made by Robert de Brus senior, Earl of Carrick and Lord of Annandale (who succeeded to Writtle in 1295) and the other two by Robert de Brus, Lord of Writtle and Lord of Annandale (i.e. the father of the above), the latter are earlier than 1295.

These three extant charters, probably typifying the others, are

---

[16] It would appear, that he had, in fact, the lordship on terms unknown, as early as 1285, i.e., during the lifetime of his father (see p. 53).

[17] D/DP T1/1770.

[18] Transcripts in E.R.O. (T/A 139, pp. 72–6).

in the form of a quitclaim or release of all services and customs in return for an annual rent.[19]   But in view of the widely varying rents for holdings of equal size and the variations in the number of services and other obligations still reserved, it would appear that each grant was individually negotiated by the tenant to get the best possible terms.

It is not possible to say with certainty from which classes of tenants the *liberi tenentes* derived: whole virgates are found among the *maiores molmanni* and *custumarii operarii;* half virgates and quarter virgates among the *minores molmanni* and *custumarii operarii;* and third parts of a virgate among the *akermanni* and *foremanni.* With regard to the virgated holdings among the four-teen whose status is not stated to derive from charters, it is pre-sumed that their privileged position antedated the lordship of the de Bruce family and rested on prescriptive right. Those holdings whose size is expressed only in acres possibly represent compara-tively late assarts. In the case of those for which the tenants had secured charters, services and customs had no doubt once been demanded and they belonged originally to the group of miscella-neous holdings dealt with below;[20]   while the remainder, for which no charters are cited, had probably always rendered a money rent and no more.

A number of these holdings are later called 'manors' and in so far as is possible these too have been plotted on Map V. But their surviving court rolls and cognate records are for the most part of comparatively late date.[21]   The absence or paucity of the records, particularly surveys and maps, inevitably means that Map V is very defective in relation to the plotting of tenements and lands which were held of these manors and which were thus removed from the tenurial structure of the Manor of Writtle itself.

It has also proved impossible in most cases to link those mesne manors to the holdings of the *liberi tenentes* given in the Extent of

[19] 'All services and customs' is somewhat modified in the *reddendo* clause which states that the reserved rent is *pro omnibus seruiciis consuetudinibus curie sectis pannagiis wardescottis auxiliis et secularibus demandis saluis nobis ac heredibus nostris et assignatis commune tallagium cum euenerit in manerio de Writele per preceptum domini regis quantum pertinet ad tantam terram eiusdem feodi et claustura parci nostri maioris de Writele quantum pertinet ad tantum tenementum.*

[20] pp. 50–1.

[21] See List of Original Sources Consulted.

1328; and some, no doubt, belonged to the third part of the manor not recorded in that document. However, as has been seen above,[22] the Manor of Wallextons is to be identified with the carucate of land held by the service of keeping the forest of Writtle.[23] The three virgates of land in the possession of William de la More and the two virgates held by William de Rolleston' in 1328 are to be identified with the Manors of Moor Hall and Rollstons respectively.

Relating the areas expressed in virgates of these two manors with their acreages given in the two 16th-century Surveys, a very considerable discrepancy is found, if the customary reckoning of 30 acres to the virgate is used. The acreage of Rollston is given as 195 and of Moor Hall 330.[24] But there is good reason to suppose that in Writtle the virgate was reckoned at 80 acres, for under the *Maiores Molmanni* the virgate of William de Barkeston' is said specifically to contain this quantity.[25] It might be considered that a single specific mention of the acreage was made because it was exceptional. But the holdings of 31 acres of arable and 1 acre of pasture, 2½ acres (of arable) and 1 acre of meadow, all shown as being part of a virgate, were in fact parcels of the virgate *quondam Ricardi atte Hegge,* a total acreage exceeding the customary quantity, and further parcels may have been allotted to the other third part of the manor.[26]

---

[22] p. 10.

[23] In 1328 it was held by John de Walexton' Thomas le Herde and his son Robert, Thomas Walexton and Roger de Merton, but the last four were no doubt cofeoffees of the first-named to his use.

[24] The quantity of Moor Hall according to two 18th-century maps and the Tithe map and award was over 460 acres, but probably includes land not originally part of the Manor.

[25] *Will(el)m(u)s de Barkeston' ten(et) vnum mes(uagium) (et) j virg(atam) t(er)re cont(inentem) iiij acras.*

[26] The lands which were the subject of the two de Bruce charters mentioned above and which belonged to the other third part of the manor were parcels of 2½ and 13 acres of a half-virgate called 'Folewell' ' or 'Folewelleshalvesyerde'; further parcels of 4 acres and 2 acres were among the holdings of the *liberi tenentes,* as well as another parcel of 10½ acres, in the 1328 Extent. The total acreage of these four parcels too is in excess of the customary 15 acres of the half-virgate.

The Maiores Molmanni

Holdings in Extent, 1328

Size	No.
1¼ virgates	1
1 virgate	3
²/₃ virgate	1
½ virgate	2
¼ virgate	1[27]

Superficially these tenants are indistinguishable from the other classes who still owed labour services to the lord. The holder of each virgate (and proportionately for the fractions of virgates) had to plough for winter seed 3 acres of demesne by the custom called 'Gauelherth' ',[28] then to sow the same with 6 bushels of heaped corn from his own stock, which he had carried to the Lord's granary to thresh and winnow, and to level off the furrows; a further acre in the same 'season' had only to be ploughed and the furrows spread after being sown with the lord's own seed by the custom called 'Benherthe',[29] which service attracted a repast of bread, ale and pottage, and an equal share in two small dishes of herring and two dishes of other unspecified fish provided for the virgater, two ploughmen and the sower. A further three acres had to be similarly ploughed, sown, etc., by the custom of 'Gauelherth' ' for Lenten sowing. While the crops were growing each virgater was obliged upon summons to weed with two men for a whole day; failure to obey the summons meant being assigned by the bailiff on the next day a specific area to be weeded, an acre of wheat. The main boonworks were naturally at harvest time. Each virgater was expected to find two men for a whole day to reap the lord's corn in return for a meal of a wheaten loaf (whereof 12 to the bushel), ale, pottage, pease, five herrings or a small dish of meat or cheese worth ½d. Failure to do this 'Custumbedrep' ' brought the more onerous task of having to reap and bind an acre

---

[27] The *compotus* of 1360–1 (D/DP M559) which relates to the whole manor gives a total of 8½ virgates held by this tenure. There were, therefore, 2⅓ virgates assigned to the other third part.

[28] For the origins of this service, see Vinogradoff, *The Growth of the Manor* (1905), pp. 225, 233, 237, 286–7, 327.

[29] *Ibid.*, pp. 234, 287.

of wheat or oat by the custom called 'Moleacres', without receiving any food or drink. By this same custom he had also to reap and to bind a further two acres of wheat and oats without sustenance being supplied. Harvest boonworks were completed with the obligation to carry nine shocks of corn from the demesne lying to the south of 'Coubreg',[30] or half as much from the fields lying to the north of the bridge. His labour services were completed with the duty to maintain ten perches of the pale of Writtle Park, for which the lord found the necessary timber in the park and had it split into pieces such as one man might carry; any old, defective pales might be kept by the repairer.

To these services were added the dues in money and kind rendered uniformly by each of the *Maiores Molmanni:* avesage for pigs owned between Michaelmas and Martinmas, at the rate of 2*d.* for each pig one year old or more by the latter feastday, 1*d.* for each six months old, ½*d.* for each three months old and 1*d.* for every four younger piglets; tallage, the impost, unspecified in amount, which the King could demand of tenants on ancient demesne at will, whether he were still lord or not; heriot, the right of the lord to the best beast on a holding upon the death of the tenant;[31] and relief, a payment by an heir (and, later on at least, by a purchaser) equal to the annual quit rent upon this entry.

It is seen that the *Maiores Molmanni,* although charged with labour services, were exempt from week work and in this lies their distinction from the other classes of tenants yet to be considered, except the *Minores Molmanni* and the miscellaneous holders of land dealt with lastly. But this relatively privileged position was not as great as that enjoyed by molmen on other manors which were not ancient demesne. At Thaxted, for example, the services

---

[30] 'Coubreg'' (Cowbridge) lies quite close to the site of the manorhouse (see Map IV).

[31] The lord's right to heriot is more fully defined in later records. It was only due in respect of a holding which had a messuage built upon it, but remained payable if the messuage were destroyed (court roll, 1634–5, E.R.O., D/DP M395); no heriot (animal or cash equivalent) could be demanded if there was no beast on the holding at the time of death or 40 days before (court roll, 1562–3, D/DP M332); only one heriot was due in the case of a property held jointly for life in survivorship (court roll, 1419–20, D/DP M224); members of the clergy were exempt from the obligation (court roll, 1466–7, D/DP M268). In the later records heriots are found to be demanded on alienation as well as death. The last heriots were rendered to the lord of Writtle in 1883 (D/DP·M420).

of the molmen elaborately described in a Survey of 1393 were never, in fact, accounted for either theoretically or actually in the bailiffs' accounts,[32] whereas at Writtle they were.[33]

The inequality of the annual quit rents is noteworthy: the 1¼ virgates rendered 7s. 7d., the virgates, 10s. 2d., 10s. and 15s. 8d. respectively, the two thirds of a virgate 3s. 4d., the two half virgates 5s. each and the quarter virgate 15d. These variations in relation to the sizes of the holdings are perhaps the result of individual bargaining in the past between the tenant and lord for the commutation of week work.

The Minores Molmanni

The Extent of 1328 lists only three holdings by this tenure— a ¼ virgate, a cottage and 3 acres of land, apparently part of a larger tenement called 'Scoureslond'', which probably was assigned to the other third part of the manor, and a messuage and 3 acres. None was called upon to do ploughing service or week work. The tenant of the ¼ virgate was charged with finding a man for a whole day to weed the lord's corn ('Bedewedyng'') when summoned, in default of which he was to reap ½ acre of corn on the morrow; with finding a man for a whole day to reap the lord's corn ('Bederepp''), for which he received the same allowance of food and drink as did the *Maiores Molmanni* or, if the summons were ignored, ½ acre of corn was to be reaped on the next day; with reaping and binding ½ acre of wheat or oats ('Molrep'') without receiving sustenance from the lord; and with repairing 2½ perches of park-pale. The two 3-acre holdings were charged with the same boon-works, but not with the upkeep of the park-pale. Quit rents amounted to 2s. for the ¼ virgate, 6d. for each of the other two tenements, and the tenants of all three were liable to be tallaged

The Custumarii Operarii

Holdings in Extent, 1328

Size	No.
1 virgate	3
½ virgate	12
¼ virgate	12[34]

[32] See my *Thaxted in the Fourteenth Century*, p. 14.
[33] D/DP M559.
[34] The *compotus* of 1360–1 (D/DP M559) gives a total of 18¼ virgates held by this tenure. There were therefore 6¼ virgates assigned to the third part of the manor not covered by the Extent, 1328.

These tenants correspond closely to those usually called virgaters and half-virgaters on other manors. The tenant of the whole virgate (and the others proportionately) performed the customary services of 'Gauelherth'' and 'Benherthe' and a 'Custumbedrep'' at harvest on the same basis as the virgater who was a *maior molmannus.* But he also had the onerous charge of doing a 'work' daily from Monday to Friday throughout the year, which the Extent divides into three customary periods—Michaelmas to Easter, Easter to St John's Day (24th June) and St John's Day to Michaelmas. The tasks which the virgater might be called upon to do in respect of his 'works' were numerous. In the period between Michaelmas and Easter, for 1 'work', he might be summoned to thresh and winnow 3 bushels of wheat, rye or pease, 6 bushels of beans and barley or 1 quarter of oats or drage; to carry by horse from Writtle to Stratford in West Ham or to some other equidistant place 2½ bushels of wheat or barley or half a quarter of oats (2 'works' being allowed if the same quantities were taken on to London or some other place of equal distance); to carry with horse and cart 8 loads of manure from the midden to the demesne land lying between the manorhouse and 'Cowbregge' or 4 cartloads to the fields beyond that bridge or 2 loads to the land beyond 'Wrytelwey'; to fell and to cart 1 load of timber from the lord's wood; to harrow one acre of land sown with oats, seeking the seed for the same at the lord's granary; to trench on open land (*terra plana*) to the length of 1 perch and width and depth of 5 feet; to scour 2 perches of ditch to a depth of 1 foot and a width of 5 feet, levelling the sides; to assist a tiler at his work on buildings for a half day (2 'works' allowed if summoned for the whole day); to make 30 perches of water-furrow at the headland or 24 perches across the middle of the demesne fields; or to do any other manual task as might be demanded, being allowed 1 'work' for a half day or 2 'works' for a whole day worked.

Between Easter and St John's Day he might be summoned to do any of the above tasks as appropriate or, additionally, also for 1 'work', to mow ½ acre of meadow and to ted the grass or to lift the hay of ½ acre of meadow and to make it into haycocks. For the period between St John's Day and Michaelmas further duties were added to this lengthy catalogue to cope with the extra labour required for the harvest, so that he might be called upon for two 'works' to carry two loads of hay with his horse and cart and two men from 'Longmed'' and 'Holmed'', one load only from 'Boyton'-fanne', which was most remote from the manorhouse, or three loads from 'Wrytelefanne', 'Hoggesmed'' or 'Vochesmad'' which lay much nearer; to reap and to bind ½ acre of wheat, oats or drage for 1 'work' or 1 acre of beans, pease or barley for 3 'works'; or to cut 80 sheaves of straw from the stubble or 5 heaps of straw of such size that the horse of the bailiff could not leap over. In common with the virgater who was a *liber tenens* or *maior mol-mannus,* the *custumarius operarius* who had this size holding was liable for the maintenance of 10 perches of the park pale. All were liable to render avesage, heriot and relief and to be tallaged. All except the holders of ¼-virgates were to serve as reeve if elected, in which event a half of their labour services was remitted.

This equality of services for all *custumarii operarii* was not matched by uniformity of rents. Two of the three whole virgates paid 3*s.* 6*d.* and 2*s.* 6*d.* respectively and the third nothing. Of the twelve ½-virgates four were wholly quit and the remainder paid sums between 5*d.* and 6*s.* 9*d.*[35] Five of the ¼-virgates were also exempt and the remaining seven paid between 5*d.* and 6*s.*[36] There was too a complete lack of pattern in the reliefs due from these holdings, which in only one case was equivalent to the annual quit rent. Thus the reliefs due from the three virgates were (with quit rents in brackets) 5*s.* (3*s.*6*d.*), 5*s.* (nothing) and 2*s.*6*d.* (2*s.*6*d.*). Among the twelve ½-virgates, three of the four which paid no quit rent were each charged with a relief of 2*s.*6*d.* and the fourth no relief; the remainder were liable for reliefs of 3*s.*1*d.* (7*d.*), 3*s.*4*d.* (10*d.*), 3*s.*9*d.* (15*d.*), 3*s.*11*d.* (5*d.*), 4*s.* (18*d.*), 5*s.*4*d.* (6*s.*9*d.*), 6*s.*6*d.* (4*s.*) and 6*s.*8*d.* (4*s.*2*d.*) respectively. Four of the five ¼-virgates which paid no quit rents were each charged with a relief of 15*d.* and the fifth with 2*d.*; the ¼-virgate from which a quit rent of 5*d.* was due was exonerated from relief, while the rest rendered 20*d.* (5*s.*), 22½*d.* (7½*d.*), 2*s.*11*d.* (20*d.*), 3*s.* (3*s.*9*d.*), 4*s.*4½*d.* (3*s.*1½*d.*) and 7*s.*3*d.* (6*s.*). The three whole virgates had also additional reliefs of 3*s.*6*d.*, 3*s.*6*d.* and 2*s.*6*d.* placed upon them in respect of unspecified parts of their lands which were

[35] 5*d.,* 7*d.,* 10*d.,* 15*d.,* 18*d.,* 4*s.,* 4*s.*2*d.* and 6*s.*9*d.*
[36] 5*d.,* 7½*d.,* 20*d.,* 3*s.*1½*d.,* 3*s.*9*d.,* 5*s.* and 6*s.*

lesignated 'Mollelond'. These possibly represent commutations of
he obligation to cultivate a part of the virgate for the direct
)enefit of the lord, but there is no other evidence to explain the
)ald statement of the Extent.

The wide variations in rents and reliefs suggest that they had
)een imposed on the holdings in piecemeal and arbitrary fashion
luring the unrecorded past as additions to the ancient uniform
labour services. Those paying no quit rent or relief possibly gained
these exemptions as a special mark of favour for some service
performed which was unconnected with the holdings.

The Akermanni

With this class of tenant there was that complete uniformity in
size of holdings, customs and services usually associated with
unfree tenure, save only that one holding in the Extent of 1328
paid a quit rent of 6*d.*, the remainder being entirely exempt,
though all were liable to a uniform relief of 20*d.* Each *aker-*
mannus, of which there are nine recorded in the Extent,[3 7] held
⅓ virgate and had to do week work on Mondays and Fridays;
and the tasks which he might be summoned to perform were the
same as those allocated to the *custumarii operarii.* In addition he
could be called upon to provide 'Custumbedripp'' at harvest-time.
At the direction of the lord any of the *akermanni* could be
appointed ploughman, in which case he was quit of all week work.
As ploughman he was responsible for the maintenance and repair of
the wooden parts of the ploughs and their yokes committed to his
custody, for which the lord provided annually from his woods five
maples and a whole ash tree with their loppings, and as much oak
as necessary for making and repairing the beams; the ironwork he
had to take to the forge for necessary attention. In return, he was
allowed the use of a demesne plough on every fourth Saturday or,
if that were a feast day, on the Saturday following. The *aker-*
mannus had also to serve as beadle, if elected, in which event he
was exonerated from all customs and services, except avesage and
tallage, for as long as he held the office; and he received as per-
quisite from the lord 1 rood of wheat and 1 rood of oats from the

[37] It is not possible to say how many belonged to the other third part of the manor, as
the various classes of tenant are not defined in the *inquisition post mortem,* 1331
(D/DP T18), and in the later records the *akermanni* are always merged with the
foremanni. It can only be deduced, therefore, that the *akermanni* and *foremanni*
belonging to the third part held among themselves 2½ virgates.

unmanured land by a custom called 'Benrode' and was allowed t
keep one of his own draught animals in the lord's pasture and t
have hay for the same.

The Foremanni

These tenants, of which seven are recorded in the Extent, si
holding ⅓ virgate and the seventh a ⅙ virgate,[38] were closel
related to the *akermanni,* for not only were their holdings, wit
one exception, of like size, but they too paid no quit rents, a fixe
relief of 20*d.*, avesage and tallage, and performed the same amoun
and kind of week work and boon work.[39] They had, howeve
different special services. Five had the duty of taking custody o
any prisoners arrested within the liberty of the manor and of cor
ducting them to the gaol at Colchester Castle. In respect of thi
guard duty an allowance of week work could be claimed at the rat
of two 'works' for each day and one 'work' for each night that
prisoner was in custody and two 'works' for the escort duty t
Colchester. The other two *foremanni* could be appointed th
lord's cowherds and shepherds, the one *ex parte Manerij de Boyton*
and the other *ex parte de Writele,* that is in the northern an
southern halves of the manor respectively. Upon appointmen
each was responsible for looking after 10 cows and 1 bul
100 ewes and 5 rams, in return for which each was permitted t
keep 2 cows and 10 sheep belonging to himself with the lord'
stock in his pasture and received a sheepskin called 'Bellewether
Fles', a lamb called 'Markyngelamb' and a rood of wheat and
rood of oats from the unmanured land. In addition each was t
make butter and cheese throughout the year finding salt for th
same; for this each received a cheese at Whitsun and could retai
all sour milk from the butter-making and all 'Pilewhay'. If eithe
tenant served as cowherd and shepherd he was released from al
week work.

The *foremanni* were also each responsible for the maintenance o
3⅓ perches of park pale, an obligation not placed upon the *aker
manni,* to whom they otherwise approximated.

Other Tenants

Immediately following the description of the *foremanni* in the

[38] See p. 49, n. 37.
[39] The ⅙ virgate was charged with half these payments and services (week work on
Fridays only), except that his liability for a boon work at harvest was not halved.

Extent there is a list of another 35 holdings, to which no collective name is given, ranging in size from a virgate to a small encroachment on the waste, some rendering labour and other services, others only a quit rent. This diversity may best be seen in the table forming Appendix D.

In the case of a number of these holdings, especially the purprestures, the smithy and other small grants of land, the reservation of only a rent in money or in kind is as expected. The two $\frac{1}{3}$ virgates were probably former tenements of *akermanni* or *foremanni*, the week work and other services of which had been commuted for the respective rents of 20*d*. (equal to the relief exacted from these tenures) and 3*s*., though the boon works of 'bedewedyng'' and 'molrepp'' still reserved were not characteristic of these tenures. In other instances it is difficult to see what really distinguished the holdings from those of the so-called *liberi tenentes*. Such is the virgate, with its obligation only to maintain 10 perches of park pale and to pay a quit rent and tallage; or the 10½ acres of arable and 2 acres of meadow which had in fact belonged to the same ½ virgate as the 4 acres and 2 acres listed under *liberi tenentes* in the Extent and as the 2½ acres and 13 acres belonging to the remainder of the manor, for which charters survive at Wadham College.[40]

Tenentes ad voluntatem domini

Lastly there were those holdings which were held at the will of the lord and which would vary in number as a result of escheat or failure of heirs or regrant. In 1328 the Bohun two-thirds of the manor had 27 properties held by this most uncertain of tenures.

Size of Holding	No.	Obligations
15 acres	1	Quit rent 15*s*.
5 acres	1	Quit rent 20*d*.
4 acres	2	(1) Quit rent 16*d*.; (2) Suit of Court twice a year.
3 acres	2	(1) Quit rent 13*d*.; (2) Avesage, heriot, tallage. Quit rent 6*d*.

[40] See p. 43, n. 26. This is further proof that the virgate in the Manor of Writtle equalled 80 acres, as the known fragments of this half-virgate amount to 34 acres.

Size of Holding	No.	Obligations
2 acres	2	(1) Quit rent 2s.;
2 acres, parcel of		(2) Quit rent 2s.
1 virgate	1	Quit rent 12d.
1½ acres	3	(1) Quit rent 6d.;
		(2) Quit rent 7½d.;
		(3) Quit rent 13½d.
1 acre 1 rood	1	Quit rent 1d.
1 acre 1 rood		
of meadow	1	Quit rent 7d.
1 acre	4	(1) Quit rent 16d.;
		(2) Quit rent 6d.;
		(3) Avesage, tallage
		and maintain
		(blank) perches
		of park pale.
		(4) Quit rent 6d.
1 acre of meadow	1	Quit rent 8d.
½ acre	2	(1) Quit rent 4d.;
		(2) Quit rent 8d.
Cottage	1	Quit rent 12d.
Purprestures	4	(1) Quit rent 1d.;
		(2) Quit rent 2d.;
		(3) Quit rent 5d.;
		(4) Quit rent 1d.
Ditch	1	Quit rent 1d.

Only three of these holdings were apparently parcels of former larger holdings: the 5 acres which are described as belonging to the land of Gerold and the 2 acres, fragment of a virgate, the residue of both of which presumably belonged to the other third part of the manor; and the 1 acre which was charged with maintaining an unspecified length of park pale and which was possibly another fragment of the ¼-virgate of which 8 acres belonged to a *liber tenens,* for they had a common former owner.

This examination of the tenurial structure and the services and other obligations of the tenants has inevitably rested heavily on the earliest available document to describe these matters in detail—the Extent of 1328. One must avoid, however, the assumption that such a document necessarily enshrines a situation wholly hallowed by 'time whereof the mind of man is not to the contrary' or gives a complete picture. The latter is certainly unlikely, for an Extent is essentially a valuation of a manor and therefore does not probably record rights and privileges upon which no cash value can be placed.

There is, however, another charter among those of Montpeliers Farm at Wadham College, made on 24 October, 10 Edward I (1285),[41] which allows the statement that the overall tenurial structure at Writtle in 1328 obtained at least as early as the 1240s, except that there was a greatly increased number of so-called *liberi tenentes* at the later date. The charter purports to be an agreement between Richard[42] de Brus, son of Lord Robert de Brus, and his tenants of the vill (*villata*) of 'Writele'. An attempt had been made to ignore the binding force of manorial custom and to place further arbitrary impositions upon the tenants, notably the *custumarii operarii*, as a result of which a plea was moved before the justices itinerant at Chelmsford.[43] Presumably de Brus was convinced of the weakness of his position and concluded the agreement; or possibly the attempt to return to arbitrary power was conceived first as a means of extortion, for in return for the charter the tenants paid the large sum of 20 *li.* and this to have *o(mn)es . . . Consuetudi(n)es q(u)as h(abe)re c(on)sueu(er)u(n)t te(m)p(or)-ib(us) Reg(is). Henr(ici) p(at)ris Reg(is) Edwardi p(re)d(i)c(t)i. (et) d(omi)ne Isabell(e) de Brus Aue p(re)d(i)c(t)i Ric(ard)i.* This perhaps illustrates that by the late 13th century the binding force of manorial custom was assured, but still at a price.

However this may be, the charter states specifically those matters about which there had been dispute and which were now resolved. It was agreed that the office of reeve should only be filled by

---

[41] 'No. 1'. Transcript in E.R.O., T/A 139, pp. 65–67.

[42] This must be a scribal error for Robert, for his grandmother is named as Isabel who held Writtle between 1241 and 1252 and there is no evidence in *The Complete Peerage, Dictionary of National Biography* or other works dealing with this family that her son Robert had a son named Richard (see also p. 41 above).

[43] *. . . cu(m) quodda(m) placitu(m) motu(m) e(ss)et int(er) p(re)d(i)c(tu)m Ric(ardum) (et) tene(n)tes p(re)d(i)c(t)os sup(er) quib(us)da(m) s(er)uic(iis) Consuetudinib(us) Acc(i)o(n)ib(us). p(er) p(re)d(i)c(tu)m Ric(ardu)m (et) tene(n)tib(us) suis p(re)d(i)c-(t)is exigitis. Coram Justiciar(iis) Itinerant(ibus) ap(u)d Chelmeresford' . . .*

MAP IV
MANOR OF WRITTLE
Demesne Lands.

A   Common Field belonging to Manor of Newarks
    in Good Easter.

B   'xvj acres in the common feilde called Newland Fee'

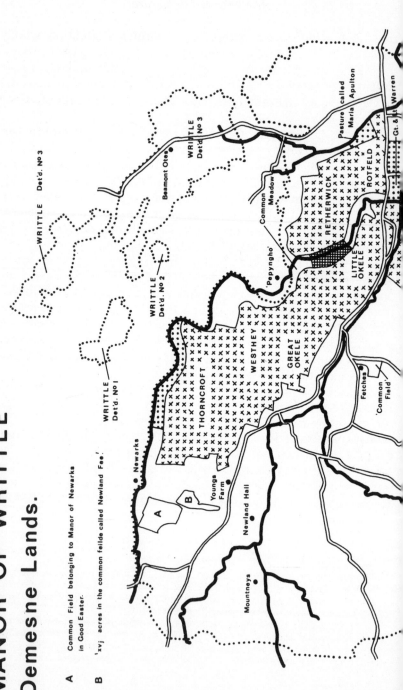

WRITTLE   Det'd. N° 3

WRITTLE
Det'd No 3

Beamont Otes

WRITTLE
Det'd. No 2

WRITTLE
Det'd. No I

Newarks

A

B

Youngs
Farm

Newland Hall

Mountneys

THORNCROFT

WESTHEY

GREAT
OKELE

Fetches

'Common
Field'

'Pepyngho'

'Common'
Meadow

RETHERWICK

LITTLE
OKELE

ROTFELD

Pasture called
Maria Apulton

Gt. & L. Warren

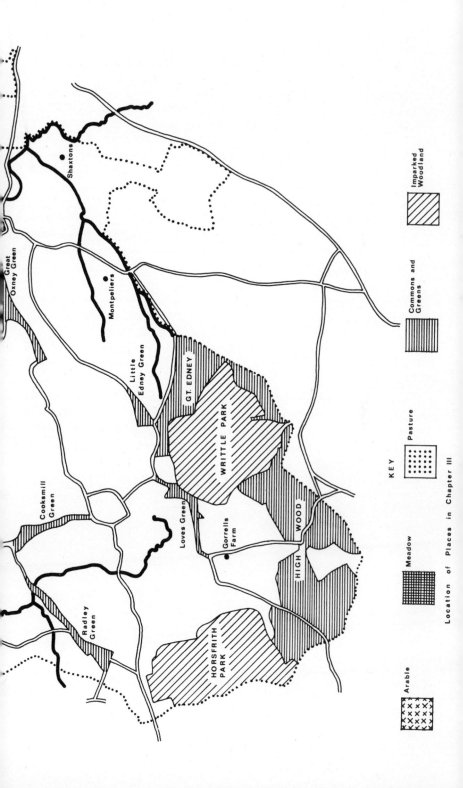

KEY

Arable

Meadow

Pasture

Commons and Greens

Imparked Woodland

Location of Places in Chapter III

Great Oxney Green

Shaxtons

Montpeliers

Little Edney Green

GT. EDNEY

Cooksmill Green

WRITTLE PARK

Loves Green

Gorrells Farm

HIGH WOOD

Radley Green

HORSFRITH PARK

customary tenants holding a whole or half virgate;[44]　the reeve for the time being should not be responsible for the arrears of his predecessors;　the customary tenants should not have to carry marl between Michaelmas and 'le Hokeday' (second Tuesday after Easter);[45]　they should not be required to thresh more than three bushels of hard corn or one quarter of oats by measure struck by hand for one 'work' or so much of other kinds of corn according to ancient custom;[46]　they should not be required to make more than 80 sheaves (of straw)[47] or 5 heaps as it was done in the time of King Henry III and Isabel de Brus;[48]　they should be summoned before the vesper hour to do their 'works' on the morrow, so that on that day they should not be put to tasks other than those for which they were first called;　and they should give 8*d.* for every acre unploughed if the lord makes no demand upon their ploughing services;[49]　and they were further granted the privilege of fishing in the rivers and streams abutting on their lands.

From one point of view, the attempt to impose the will of the lord unfettered by the custom of the manor seems at variance with the 'liberalising' de Brus charters creating the so-called *liberi tenentes.*　Possibly, however, they are the two sides of a single coin—the acquisition of ready money by single comparatively large sums rather than depending only on the annual income from the smaller amounts derived from rents and services, or by any other means to hand.

---

[44] The Extent, 1328, restricts the office to *custumarii operarii* holding a whole or half virgate (see p. 48 above).

[45] Such a service does not appear in the Extent.

[46] The specific quantities accord with those given in the Extent (see p. 47 above).

[47] See p. 48 above.

[48] For the method of determining the size of the heaps, see p. 48.

[49] This accords with the Extent.

V

CULTIVATION OF THE DEMESNE FOR THE LORD

On the evidence which has survived Writtle conformed to the general pattern of mixed farming in the Chelmsford Hundred with the production of corn predominant, but with the rearing of sheep also having an important place in the economy. This was true at Domesday and was no less true in the 14th century. If the redistribution of the land among lord and tenants discussed in Chapter III took place after 1086 it made little or no difference to this pattern.

Unfortunately detailed knowledge of the working of demesne while it was still being cultivated directly for the lord rests on a single bailiff's account of 1360–1.[1] There is a further account of 1366–7,[2] but by that date a large part of the demesne was already leased and the document contains other untypical features, so that its use to give a picture of demesne farming on the 'classical' model is small. A series of other *compoti* covering much of the 15th century[3] relate to the period when the manor was being leased in its entirety and these do not in fact give any real indication of the way the demesne was being worked by the farmer and do not therefore provide a · basis of comparison with the account of 1360–1.

As has been seen, the demesne arable lay in at least seven large fields and two small enclosures, but the *seisona* not the field was the areal unit of husbandry. Each of the three *seisone* might overlap from one field into the next or account for only part of the total acreage of a field, forming not a homogenous area of arable but separate blocks. The importance of this division of the land is illustrated by the fact that it was maintained when there was a physical partitioning of the land between de Bohun and de Waleys in the period 1296 to 1331[4] and was continued, with necessary reallocation of land to the three *seisone,* when the demesne was farmed as a single unit again. Writtle was in short a typical three-course rotation manor.

---

[1] D/DP M559.
[2] D/DP M560.
[3] D/DP M561–592.
[4] See pp. 23–7 above.

Analysis of the 1360—1 bailiff's account shows that at that date
the three *seisone* were made up as follows:—

		Acreages
First 'Seisona' (winter-sown crops)		
In Westhey		196
In Alfaresfeld		84
	Total	280

Second 'Seisona' (spring-sown crops)		
In Westhey		16
In Thorncroft		196
In Rotfeld		11
In (Great) Bradfeld		66½
In Little Bradfeld		9½
In Alfaresfeld		13
	Total	312

Third 'Seisona' (fallow)		
In Westhey		22
In Rotfeld		90
In 'Okele' (Great and Little Okele)		320[5]
	Total	432

The disproportionate amount of land apparently lying fallow
suggests that something like 100—150 acres of 'Okele' was
permanently out of cultivation at this time, as was the elusive
136 acres which had belonged to the de Waleys third part of the
manor prior to 1331,[6] and the small enclosure called Barleycroft.
The bailiff's account of 1360—1 offers no evidence that these lands
were being leased or used as pasturage.

Almost the whole limited range of main crops available to the
medieval farmer was grown at Writtle. In 1360—1 the distribution
of the crops was:—

Winter-Sown (First 'Seisona')

Wheat	196 acres in Westhey
	52 acres in Alfaresfeld
	248 acres

---

[5] The acreage of 'Okele' is not given in the 1360—1 bailiff's account. The figure of
320 acres is the combined figures for Great Okele and Little Okele appearing in the
1328 Extent.

[6] See p. 24, n. 5.

Winter-Sown (First 'Seisona')

| Maslin (mixture of wheat and rye) | 32 acres in Alfaresfeld |

Spring-Sown (Second 'Seisona')

Barley
  16 acres in Westhey
  3½ acres in (Great) Bradefeld
  13 acres in Alfaresfeld
  ─────────
  32½ acres

Oats
  144½ acres in Thorncroft
  11 acres in Rotfeld
  56 acres in (Great) Bradefeld
  ─────────
  211½ acres

Peas
  14 acres in Thorncroft
  3 acres in (Great) Bradefeld
  ─────────
  17 acres

Benemong (mixture of beans and peas)
  24 acres in Thorncroft
  4 acres in (Great) Bradefeld
  ─────────
  28 acres

Bolymong (mixture of beans or peas and oats)
  13½ acres in Thorncroft

Drage (mixture of oats and barley)
  9½ acres in Little Bradefeld

The relative acreages of each seed sown was no doubt dictated mainly by demand, but the particular suitability of the soil for certain of the grains may well have been an important factor. The sowing of 2¼ bushels of wheat and a tiny fraction under 3 bushels of oats per acre were below the averages of 2½–3 bushels for the former and 4¼ bushels for the latter grain generally accepted;[7] whereas the sowing of 4 bushels of barley per acre was above the average of 3¾ bushels. By any standard the amount of oats required was very economical. That these quantities of oats and

---

[7] Thorold Rogers, *History of Agriculture and Prices in England, 1259–1400* (1866), i, p. 56; W. Beveridge, 'The Yield and Price of Corn in the Middle Ages' in *Economic Journal* (Supplement), May 1927. See also H. S. Bennett, *Life on the English Manor, 1150–1400 (1938)*, pp. 86–7.

barley per acre were normal in Writtle is evidenced by the bailiff's account for 1376–7.[8] The figures for maslin and drage conform to those of the constituent grains when grown singly (except rye which was not grown as an individual crop).

The paucity of evidence does not allow any real attempt to estimate the average yield of the crops, though the known quality of the soil no doubt meant that in good years the generally accepted averages of around 10 bushels per acre for wheat and oats and 14 bushels for barley were comfortably achieved. The 1360–1 account gives the yields of the 1360 harvest (see Appendix E) for which the bailiff answered, but the exact acreages from which each crop was derived are in most cases unknown; nor does it allow for tithe which was taken in the field and was not therefore accounted for by the bailiff who became responsible for the grain only after it reached the grange.[9] Allowing for tithe it would appear that a little over 235 quarters of wheat and 13¾ quarters of maslin were produced from the 312 acres in Westhey, Thorncroft, Rotfeld, Great and Little Bradfeld and Alfaresfeld which formed the first *seisona* in that year. This represents a yield of only 6¼ to 6½ bushels to the acre, representing a below-average harvest, which did not reach the threefold increase specified by Walter of Henley as essential for profitability, though he qualifies it by adding, unless the price was high, as indeed it was.[10]

Using the figures set out in Appendix E less specifically a more general picture of the spade-husbandry of the manor may be composed, though the quality of the harvests in 1360 and 1361 must always be borne in mind for their possible distorting influences. It is seen that only the main crops of wheat, barley and oats were grown in sufficient quantity to allow large surpluses for sale outside the manor; only small quantities of the other crops were so available. After allowing for grain used for seed, domestic needs on the manor, the principal purchasers were the household of the lord[11] and the anonymous merchants; the small sales *super*

---

[8] The quantity of wheat sown cannot be checked as none was grown for the 1377 harvest.

[9] See R. Lennard in *Economic Journal* (Supplement), February, 1936.

[10] *Walter of Henley's Husbandry* . . . ed. E. Lamond (Royal Historical Society, 1890), p. 19. For the high price of corn in 1360–1, see pp. 59–60 below.

[11] In 1360–1 Humphrey de Bohun, Earl of Hereford and Essex.

compotum were no doubt made to local inhabitants of Writtle or, more likely, represent quantities for which the bailiff was unable to account.

The income from sales in 1360–1 is of some interest. Summarised it was

Lord's household	li.	s.	d.
39 qrs. of wheat (sold at divers prices)	12.	6.	0.
12 qrs. 6 bus. of bolymong	2.	2.	6.
123 qrs. of oats	15.	11.	4.
9 qrs. of maslin	2.	2.	0.
	32.	1.	10.

Merchants			
20 qrs. of wheat to merchants at Stratford (at 9s. 6d. a qr.)	9.	10.	0.
10 qrs. of wheat to other merchants (at 9s. a qr.)	4.	10.	0.
43 qrs. of barley to other merchants (at 6s. 8d. a qr.)	14.	6.	8.
7 qrs. 5 bus. of drage to other merchants (at 4s. a qr.)	1.	10.	6.
	29.	17.	2.

The demands of the manor and the lord's household took the whole of the available oats, bolymong and maslin. The absence of any demand by the household for barley is possibly accounted for by its provision by other manors belonging to the great complex of Bohun estates. It is worthy of note, in the one case where there is a basis of direct comparison, that although the household made payment for the wheat received, instead of it being regarded as a free quota, the average price (6s. 1.85d.) was only about two thirds of that paid by the merchants. The market price was extremely high in this period of poor or disastrous harvests.[12] The additional 6d. per quarter paid for wheat by the merchants at Stratford probably reflects transportation costs and their nearness to London

---

[12] The average price of wheat between 1261 and 1400 was 5s. 10¾d., but the 14th century saw two periods of relatively very high prices attributable principally to poor harvests. The decenniel average price of wheat for 1311–20 and 1361–70 was 7s. 11d.

where a higher price might be expected to rule than within the County itself.

The very high price of wheat suggests at first sight a dearth as a result of a particularly bad harvest in 1360. Certainly the quantities of grain available for sale in 1360—1 indicate that the yields were well below average. There is extant one other set of figures for sales of grain, dating from 1230[13] which make an interesting if not very significant comparison.

	1230	1360—1
Wheat	188 qrs.	69 qrs.
Oats	220	127⅝
Barley	–	43¹/₁₆
Rye	42½	–
Maslin	–	9
Bolymong	–	13
Drage	–	8⅛
Peas	5	6⅝
Benemong	–	2⁷/₁₆
Dross-wheat	3	–
Dross-rye	4	–

There are obviously too many unknowns for absolute conclusions to be drawn. But it is likely in 1230 that the yield was from an acreage representing around three quarters of the demesne arable, for the sheriff accounted for *11 li. viijs. de quibusdam operationibus manerij positis ad firmam.*, which sum is just under one third of the total value of the ploughing and sowing services and 'works'.[14] The implication from this and in particular from the use of the term *ad firmam* is that a proportionate amount of the demesne was then being leased. As will be seen,[15] a comparable area was on lease in 1376—7. The figures for 1230, therefore, are indicative of the comparatively poor 'export' quantities in 1360—1.

One is confronted, however, by the large surplus of the grain answered for by the bailiff when he closed his account at Michaelmas, 1361. Of the total of 101 quarters left over only 27

---

[13] *Pipe Roll, 14 Henry III* (Pipe Roll Society, N.S.4, 1927), pp. 162—3, in the account of the Sheriff of Essex as keeper of the manor on behalf of the King.

[14] Calculated from the bailiff's account, 1376—7, where the cash value of all the labour obligations is given.

[15] See pp. 68—9.

represented the first receipts from the 1361 harvest still in progress; the rest came from the crop of the previous year. While the indications are that the 1360 harvest was below average this was not the principal cause of the high price. Rather was it the withholding of stocks from the market at the prospect of a worse, even calamitous, harvest in 1361. There is no direct reference to such a failure in the bailiff's account, but it makes clear that the hay harvest was of this nature as a result of the great dryness of the summer; and records that nothing was received from the hire of the ploughs for the same reason.[16] It would appear therefore that the large surplus of wheat seed retained was the result of foresight and was to stand the manor in good stead for the sowing of the 1362 harvest.

In this period of poor crops, it is also apparent from the bailiff's account that the demesne arable was being cultivated well below its full potential, even by the standards of medieval husbandry. Out of its 1,269 acres only 1,024, and probably 100–150 acres less than this, were in cultivation, including the land lying fallow as part of the three-course system of rotation. As has been seen this is a comparable acreage to that being worked directly for the lord in 1230, but in that year the rest was leased; in 1360–1 it must have been lying derelict.

The working of the manor in 1360–i was still carried on without the employment of paid day-labourers, for the bailiff's account records no expenditure on wages. None of the ploughing services ('Gauelherthe' and 'Benherthe'), however, were done by the *Maiores Molmanni* and *Custumarii Operarii*. In theory the holders of the 26¾ virgates belonging to these tenures were liable to plough 26¾ acres in each of the first and third *seisone* and to plough, to sow and to harrow a further 80¼ acres in each of the first and second *seisone*. But these services had been sold to the tenants of 25¾ virgates and those holding the remaining virgate (made up of a half virgate and two quarter virgates) were paying enhanced quit rents in lieu of all services. These primary operations of the farming year were being done by the *akermanni* charged with the office of ploughman and the four ploughmen numbered among the

---

[16] The account states that only 27 acres of meadow were mown at the first cut *Et no(n) plur(ies) q(uia) vj acr(e) d(imidia) in Longemad iij acr(e) in Hogges mad ij acr(e) in Fochesmad (et) iij acr(e) in Holemad non falc(untur) sed depascunt(ur) cu(m) bob(is) vacc(is) (et) aliis au(er)ijs Man(er)ij p(r)o mag(n)a siccit(ate) in estate hoc anno;* and *De caruc(is) loc(atis) n(ihi)l hoc anno p(ro) magna siccitate estate.*

famuli, with the help of three lads who following behind the sowers covered the furrows.[17]

It will be noted, however, that even if the customary ploughing etc., had been fully utilised it would only have accounted for about one sixth of the whole demesne arable or between one quarter and one fifth of the acreage actually under cultivation in 1360–1. And even if all the virgated holdings held by the so-called *liberi tenentes* had formerly performed these services, the greater part of the demesne arable must always have been ploughed by men belonging to the *famuli*. Whereas in 1086 there had been 9 ploughs on the demesne and 12 in 1066, the work in 1360–1 could be coped with by 4 ploughs, to which were assigned 24 stotts, 16 oxen and 4 horses (of which two were weak). These figures for the numbers of ploughs are no doubt testimony to the greater efficiency of the ploughteam in the 14th century compared with that of the 11th century. That the four ploughs in 1360–1 were sufficient is borne out by the fact that it was normally possible to hire them out when not required for ploughing the demesne. The comparatively large number of draught animals assigned to the ploughs is, of course, not an indication of the number and type of animal assigned to and used by each team at one time, despite the apparent significance of the figures being each divisible by four, but were such as to provide always a fresh team for each plough and perhaps combinations of different animals to suit different soil and weather conditions.[18]

Because no threshing and winnowing of seed was carried out by the custom of 'Gauelherthe', these tasks fell wholly upon the *custumarii operarii, akermanni* and *foremanni* as part of their week work, as is stated in the section of the account dealing with grain stocks.[19] Unfortunately it lacks the detailed statement of

---

[17] *In lib(eracione) ij Carect(ariorum) iiij fugator(um) caruc(arum) ij vaccar(iorum) (et) j Bercar(ij) p(er) a(nnu)m xxxviij q(u)ar(terij) vj b(usselli) [d(imidius) b(ussellus) interlined]. In lib(eracione) iij garc(i)o(n)um sp(er)g(antium) sulcos in seisona fr(ument)i j q(u)ar(terius) iij b(usselli) fr(ument)i.*

[18] The horse could plough more quickly but was more expensive to keep; the ox was cheaper to feed and was also more valuable for his meat and hide when his working life was over, but he was, in addition to being slower, less sure-footed. Walter of Henley counselled a team of two horses and two oxen. (See Thorold Rogers, *Six Centuries of Work and Wages* (1884), p. 76). There was possibly a deficiency of horses in 1360–1, for in 1376–7 when the number of demesne ploughs had fallen to one the same proportion of stotts and oxen was maintained (i.e. six and four) but there were two horses.

[19] e.g. *Et de v. q(u)ar(teriis) ij b(ussellis) de exit(u) grang(ie) ib(ide)m mens(ura) ras(a) tr(iticatis) p(er) op(er)a.*

'works' owed and actually performed or sold which normally appears on the dorse of such accounts, although the numbers sold do appear on the face of the document where income is itemised. However, using the account of 1376–7 to establish the nominal total of 'works' due, the Extent of 1328 for their nature and certain automatic deductions, and a List of Saint Days and the dates on which they fell,[20] it is possible to reconstruct in some measure the missing figures and these have been embodied in Appendix F.

It is seen that even if week work was fully exacted the burden on the three classes of tenants from which it was due was not as heavy as a superficial reading of the 1328 Extent would suggest. The remission of 'works' for feast days obviously varied a little from year to year, particularly in the case of the *akermanni* and *foremanni* who worked only on Mondays and Fridays. But overall about one fifth of 'winter works', nearly one sixth of 'summer works' and something more than one tenth of 'autumn works' might be expected to be never done for this reason. In addition the 'works' of the two *akermanni* serving as beadle and ploughman and of the two *foremanni* acting as shepherds and cowherds were also to be subtracted.

In the farming year 1360–1, when only about two thirds to three quarters of the demesne arable was being cultivated, the number of 'works' actually available was more than adequate. After allowing for those of the five holdings now paying money rents in lieu of services there were surpluses of 872½ winter, 568⁵/₁₂ summer and 317 autumn 'works' which were sold. Relating these figures to the total actually due, it would seem that even when the whole demesne was under cultivation there was always a surplus of winter and summer 'works' which could either be utilised on those tasks indirectly associated with cultivation[21] or sold. The large number of summer 'works' sold in 1360–1 is probably unusually large as a result of the partial failure of the hay crop. In the autumn period, however, the figures indicate that there is unlikely to have been a surplus, unless there was a failure of the crops, illustrating the importance of the boon works ('Custumbedrepe' and 'Molrepe') as a supplementary pool of labour at harvest-time. Their import-

[20] *Handbook of Dates for Students of English History,* ed. C. R. Cheney (Royal Historical Society Guides and Handbooks, No. 4, 1948).
[21] See p. 47.

ance is underlined by the fact that in 1361, despite the surplus of
autumn 'works' all tenants owing 'Custumbedrepe' were summoned to find the necessary men.[22]   Whether 'Bedeweding' and
'Molrepes' were also exacted is unknown for they were 'dry'
services (i.e. no food or drink was provided by the lord), and in
the absence of the account of 'works' this cannot be ascertained
as in the case of 'Custumbedrepes' where food was given.

It was, no doubt, more advantageous to exact boon works than
week work,[23] for as the Extent of 1328 states specifically, the
former was for *unum diem integrum* whereas week work was based
on a half day's labour and would entail organising two teams of
men each day during harvesting.[24]

Only in one aspect can it be deduced exactly how the regular
week work was shared out in 1360–1 among the various tasks
described in the 1328 Extent. Relating the amounts of grain to be
threshed and winnowed for one 'work' given in the Extent to the
quantities recorded in the bailiff's account, it is found that 988½
out of the 1,479½ winter 'works' were spent on these tasks.

As mentioned previously, although Writtle was primarily one of
the corn-producing manors of central Essex, the rearing of sheep
played a significant part in its economy. The comparatively large
number at the time of Domesday has been noticed and that this
characteristic continued thereafter is evidenced by the assignment
of the position of shepherd to two of the *foremanni* and by the
stock account in the bailiff's account, 1360–1, though the flock
neither at Domesday nor in the 14th century was, of course, as
large as those on the marshland manors of Essex.[25]

The details of livestock, summarised in Appendix G, shows that
sheep-rearing was the one element in the economy of Writtle which

---

[22] By the custom the labour of 102 men each working for a whole day was the nominal
amount available, but the five holdings paying enhanced quit rents in lieu of services
reduced the number of men to 96. The wheat account records that bread for this
number was provided.

[23] 'As a rule, though not invariably, the boon-services were commuted last of all'
(E. Lipson, *The Economic History of England*, vol. i, revised edition, 1937, p. 90).

[24] It is true that work connected with harvesting is expressed in amount of work to be
done, not time to be spent, but that the amount was considered the equivalent of a
half day's labour is borne out by the other tasks which are expressed in terms of time
(e.g. he shall serve a tiler for a half day for 1 work or for 1 day for 2 works).

[25] On the Manor of Foulness (on Foulness Island) in 1424–5 there were 2,295 sheep
of which 92 were rams, 1,602 ewes and 400 new-born lambs. (Bailiff's account
D/DK M135).

was inter-related with those of other manors in the Bohun complex of estates in Essex. Thus 140 new lambs were received from John Hamond, reeve of the neighbouring Manor of (Great) Waltham, and 80 year-old lambs from Ralph Coby, servant at 'le Roos' in the Manor of Walden in the north-west of the County;[26] from Writtle went 39 gimmers to Great Waltham and 110 year-old lambs and 8 *multoni* to Foulness Island.

The sheep was a multi-purpose animal. First and foremost it provided that staple commodity of medieval England—wool; for which reason the bailiff of the manor was always careful to record whether deaths from murrain and sales and purchases occurred before or after shearing, so that his tally of fleeces accorded exactly with the number of sheep at the time of the clip. Scarcely of less value was the manure which the flock laid upon the arable land as it grazed on the stubble and the fallow.[27] But even a comparatively large flock could not adequately manure a great area of arable as at Writtle. For one thing the amount of grazing provided there did not allow the flock to be left on the fields sufficiently long and it had to be moved on, even to the roadside verges in a year of poor pasturage as in 1361.[28] And some arable had always to remain unmanured, for the Extent of 1328 specifies that the *akermannus* who shall be elected beadle of the manor shall receive from the lord 1 rood of wheat and 1 rood of oats from the unmanured land by the custom called 'Benrod' '.[29] The sheep also provided meat, though this was a comparatively small part of their overall importance at Writtle. Their fourth function was the provision of milk by the ewes during the summer to supplement that provided by the cows. Camden in the last edition of his *Britannia* (1607) emphasises the importance of this aspect of sheep-farming in relation to the flocks populating the Essex marshlands.

In 1360—1 the dairy side of the economy was leased on an annual basis to an unnamed farmer. For the milking of 205 ewes during the summer 2*d.* per head was paid; and for the milking and calving

[26] For the importance of sheep-farming at Saffron Walden, see *The Fields of Saffron Walden in 1400*, by D. Cromarty (E.R.O. Publications, No. 43).

[27] *De pastur(a) cheuett(e) (et) t(er)re frisc(e) in Okle n(ihi)l q(uia) depasci(tur) cu(m) bidenc(ibus) d(omi)ni hoc anno.*

[28] *De past(ur)a in Admondestrat n(ihi)l q(uia) depascit(ur) cu(m) bid(encibus) d(omi)ni hoc anno.*

[29] *... et p(er)cip(iet) de d(omi)no rod(am) fr(ument)i (et) j rod(am) auen(e) de t(er)ra non compost(a) de cons(uetudine) vocat(a) Benrode ...*

of 58 cows and 3 heifers 6s. 4d. per head. The farmer was apparently obliged to sell any calves to the lord as required, for the purchase of 8 heifers for 22s. from him is recorded in the account. The small numbers of geese (at 12d. each) and cocks and hens (at 6d. each) were similarly let out.[30]

With only one defective bailiff's account extant relating to the period when the demesne was being cultivated wholly for the lord, and that belonging to an abnormal farming year, it is impossible to give any certain idea of the average profitability of the manor, but a break-down of the sources of income in the following form illustrates a number of points of general application:—

(i)	li. s. d.	(ii)	li. s. d.
Issues of the Manor	10. 7. 0.	Rents of Assize	40. 15. 2¼
Sale of corn	61. 19. 0.	Rents in kind	2. 2.
Sale of livestock	10. 16. 4.	Market and fairs	6. 8.
Dairy	21. 10. 8.	Custom called 'Lepeseluer'[31]	6. 8.
Sales upon the account	4. 17. 3½	Custom called 'Leseseluer'[32]	9. 0.
	109. 10. 3½	Avesage	2. 12. 0½
		Lease of tenants' lands	6. 11.11½
		Sale of works and customs	13. 11. 3¼
		Perquisites of courts	14. 11. 7½
			79. 6. 7.

The two columns divide the sources of income into (i) those arising from the direct farming operations and (ii) those derived from the privileged status of the estate as a manor.

It is seen that on a large manor such as Writtle the income from 'manorial' sources formed a significant proportion of the total, even allowing for the income from farming being probably on the low side in 1360—1. Provided that a series of catastrophic harvests did not pauperise the tenants preventing them from paying their quit rents and customary payments, amercements and fines, the 'manorial' sources always ensured an income greater than expendi-

---

[30] It was common for such animals and poultry to be leased to others, particularly those given to churches for the maintenance of obits and lights.

[31] 'Lepeseluer' was a customary payment of 2d. by those dwelling about the seven commons of Greenbury, Oxney, Highwood, Arnswick (Cooksmill), Radwell and Newney who had four-footed animals between Michaelmas and Martinmas; and by strangers driving four-footed animals and carts across the same commons during the same period, only the long carts of magnates being exempt (See Extent, 1328).

[32] 'Leseseluer' was a further annual payment of 2d. on the Feast of the Nativity of St. John the Baptist by the same dwellers about the commons having quadrupeds.

ture normally incurred. The showing of a surplus on the account was independent of the quality of the harvest; this only determined how large the surplus was to be.

In the 1360—1 bailiff's account only the following heads of expenditure are given:—

	li.	s.	d.
A payment of rent by the lord to the heirs of a tenant			6.
Deductions and allowances of rents[33]		19.	5.
Cost of ploughs	4.	0.	0.
Cost of carts	1.	14.	9.
Necessaries (including cost of repair of buildings)	1.	18.	4.
Purchase of livestock	2.	18.	4.
Cost of parks		9.	9.
Cost of (water-)mill	3.	17.	10.
Cost of the sheep		16.	4½
	16.	15.	3½

By comparison with the 1376—7 account the missing portion of the roll must have contained the annual wages of the *famuli* (which in 1376—7 amounted to 1*li*. 12*s*. 8*d*.) and the bailiff (2*li*. 16*s*. 8*d*.), the expenses of the steward and auditors (1*li*. 8*s*. 0*d*.) and 'forinsec' expenses. Clearly the last two items were not fixed sums and the 'forinsec' expenses could vary very widely from year to year.[34] But allowing for this and other obvious variations in costs, such as repairs of buildings, purchase of stock, etc., the Manor of Writtle in 1361, still working on the 'classical' model if well below its potential and in a period of poor harvests, was a highly profitable estate to possess.

Yet by 1376 the relatively unchanging picture presented by the bailiff's account for 1361-2 was in the process of radical alteration.

---

[33] These are, of course, not strictly expenditure but are allowances and deductions in respect of tenants' holdings leased or unoccupied and should therefore be subtracted from the income from the rents of assize and farm of tenants' land for which the bailiff answered.

[34] In 1376—7, for example, the ancient annual charge of 4*d*. a day to the monks of 'Bergh' in Writel'' (Bedemansberg) was not paid 'quia nulli monach(i) ib(ide)m fuer(ant) hoc a(nn)o'; this may have been paid in 1360—1. On the other hand, expenses incurred in a plea heard in the Exchequer between Joan de Bohun, Countess of Hereford, Essex and Northampton, Lady of the manor, and the King concerning Horsfrith Park, amounting to 8*li*. 8*s*. 4*d*. was an *ad hoc* charge; it included 40*s*. in gifts given to 12 men sworn on the inquisition 'p(ro) eor(um) bona volunt(ate) h(ab)end(a)', gifts to officers of the Exchequer and sergeants and presents to the Barons of the Exchequer as breakfasts and drinks 'p(ro) dict(is) negoc(iis) exped(iendis)'. A similar 'once only' expense was 18*s*.4*d*. paid in the expenses of household servants and other men from Evesfield and Barnet (both Bohun manors), who came to Writtle in June 1377 and stayed for 1 night, breakfasting on the morrow before going on to 'Badewe' (Great Baddow) to avenge the injury done to Richard Herde, the lady's bondman there, by the servants of Lord Hugh de Badewe. It would appear that a full-scale local war was intended

MAP V

Lands of other Chief Manors and Sub-Manors in the ancient Parish of Writtle.

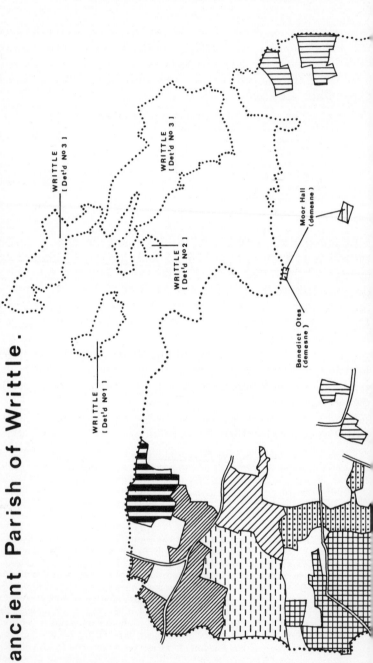

WRITTLE
(Det'd No 3)

WRITTLE
(Det'd No 3)

WRITTLE
(Det'd No 2)

WRITTLE
(Det'd No 1)

Moor Hall
(demesne)

Benedict Otes
(demesne)

CHIEF MANORS

Newland Hall (demesne)
Newland Hall (freeholds)
Romans Fee (demesne)
Romans Fee (freeholds)

Moor Hall (demesne)
Skreens (demesne)
Shakestons (demesne)
Newarks (demesne)

Moor Hall (freeholds)
Fithlers (demesne)
Benedict Otes (demesne)

Tye Hall (demesne)
Wallextons (demesne)

SUB-MANORS

Montpeliers (demesne)

Rollstons (demesne)

Skreens (freeholds)

Mountnays (demesne)

VI

THE ELEMENTS OF CHANGE

A lthough Writtle still maintained most of the essential characteristics of the old manorial economic order in 1361, it was to experience during the next decade and a half the beginnings of the break up of that order, whereby the elements of 'natural' economy—the performance of labour and other services— were replaced, though not quickly, by a single element, money. It is proposed first to describe the form which this transformation took and then to examine discernible factors involved.[1]

The lord of a manor faced with the need or desirability, for whatever reasons, to abandon the direct cultivation of his demesne had two courses open to him: either to alienate the land to another or others, i.e. to dispossess himself entirely of his freehold, or to lease it for a term of years, receiving an agreed annual rent from the lessee(s). The former entailed the commutation of labour services due from his manorial tenants; the latter not necessarily so. At Writtle, the latter course was adopted without any general commutation of services initially.

By 1376 an intermediate stage had been reached. The demesne lands at Boyton (i.e. lying in Roxwell and comprised in the present-day Boyton Hall and Little Boyton Hall farms) were leased to John atte Wode, one of the more affluent tenants of the manor. The remainder of the demesne was to some extent still being worked directly for the lady.[2] The account rolls of John atte Wode as 'farmer' of the Boyton lands have not survived, but the bailiff's accounts for 1376–7[3] shows that his lease included the assignment to him of the ploughing services and week work of 8 *Shokmanni (Custumarii Operarii)* holding together 4½ virgates and the week work of 10 *Foremanni* who held 3 virgates, as well as their harvest

---

[1] No reference will be made to the Peasants' Revolt, for there is no evidence that it spread to Writtle. It may be felt, however, that the fact that the court rolls, with a single exception, begin in 1382 is significant; though it is possible that the earlier rolls were at the time not in Writtle but elsewhere and so were destroyed.

[2] Joan de Bohun, Countess of Hereford, Essex and Northampton.

[3] D/DP M560. The account covers only from 16 December (instead of the customary 30 September) 1376 to 29 September 1377 apparently as a result of a change of bailiff.

boonworks. Unfortunately, the account gives no further information about the terms of the lease, except that the lessee was supplied with 5 quarters of oats without making payment.

It does show, however, that the demesne still retained by the lady was only under partial cultivation, for it records only the following crops and acreages sown:—

Peas	4½ acres in Alfaresfeld (2½ bushels to the acre)
'Pesemong'	4½ acres in Alfaresfeld (3 bushels to the acre)
Barley	5 acres in Little Bradefeld (4 bushels to the acre)
Drage	5 acres in Little Bradefeld
	6 acres in Alfaresfeld (4 bushels to the acre less 4 bushels overall)
Oats	81 acres in Alfaresfeld (3 bushels to the acre less 1 bushel overall)

As the arable under lease accounted for 545½ acres,[4] there remained for direct cultivation 743½ acres; yet only 106 acres or little more than one fifth (allowing for the fallow in the three course system) was under crops. These did not include the usual winter-sown wheat and maslin in the first *seisona*. The bailiff's account records only the issue of small quantities of these grains as payments, gifts and one small sale and an unknown amount of wheat[5] and 30 quarters of maslin lying unthreshed in the stack. It offers no hint of the reason for this run-down state of the demesne still in hand.

The position in the next twenty years is difficult to determine as there are no account rolls of either bailiffs or lessees, but the record of amercements for failure to perform labour services and trespass in standing crops suggests that the Boyton land continued to be leased, while the remainder of the demesne continued to be cultivated, in whatever degree, directly for the lady.

In 1397, the whole manor, with certain reservations, was leased to Ralph Rede, who was also farming the adjoining Bohun manors of Chignal and Mashbury, for a period of 15 years. His account roll for the seventh year of his term (1403—4) survives[6] and

---

[4] The fields called Thorncroft (196 acres), Westhey (234 acres) and Great Okele (in so far as it lay *ex parte Boyton'*) (115 acres). The acreage of the last field is given in the 'farmer's' account for 1417—8 (D/DP M562).

[5] Unknown because illegible even with the aid of ultra-violet light.

[6] D/DP M561.

indicates that his lease reserved to the lady wardships, marriages, escheats, fees, advowsons, Writtle and Horsfrith Parks with the custom of fencing them, wood and underwood and the profit of the warren, the manorhouse within the moat, stables, the 'Gathous' and a certain building before the bridge beyond the moat, waived chattels, the chattels of felons and fugitives, and strays exceeding in value in one year 40 shillings; it assigned to Rede all other demesne lands, buildings and the perquisites of courts.

Under the terms of the lease, Rede had to answer for the income from those sources reserved to the lady. Thus, in 1403–4, in addition to his annual rent of 146*li.* 13*s.* 4*d.,* he accounted for 19*s.* 10*d.* from pannage in the two parks, 17*s.* 10*d.* from the sale of underwood in Highwood and 2*li.* 12*s.* from mares and foals sold from the parks.[7] Items from which there was no income in that year—sale of faggots and other wood and conies and agistment of beasts in the parks—are carefully recorded. He was also responsible for the usual annual allowance of wheat and salaries paid to the warrener and to the woodward of Highwood, the salaries of the parkers of Writtle and Horsfrith Parks and the cost of maintaining the parks including the lodges and other buildings in them; but all these charges, except half the payments to the warrener and woodward, were deducted from his annual rent.[8] He also paid, but debited similarly, the cost of all repairs to the manorhouse and other buildings on the demesne and the erection of new ones[9] and for the purchase of miscellaneous items which might arise under *expense forincece.*[10] It will be observed that the principle of a self-sufficient estate noticed when the manor was being cultivated directly for the lord was carried over into the period of leasing.

None of the leases granted survive, but sufficient of the lessees' annual account rolls are extant[11] to show that the manor, with

[7] There is evidence that earlier the parks were also used as a stud by Edward, 'the Black Prince'. See Pipe Roll 169, 17 Edward II (1323–4), and F. H. Pavry and G. M. Knocker, 'The Mount, Princes Risborough' (*Records of Buckinghamshire,* 1957–8, pp. 133–78).

[8] In 1403–4 they amounted to 7*li.*19*s.*7*d.*

[9] In 1403–4 only 24*s.*3*d.*

[10] In 1403–4 these included payment to a tenant of a 'formanlond' and part of a virgate of 10*s.*6*d.,* the value of his works and services released to him by the lady *p(ro) sua impotencia c(aus)a lesionis cu(m) j falce metent(e) blad(ium) d(omi)ne in antu(m)pno;* and 10*s.* being the lady's moiety of the payment of the subsidy granted by Parliament to the King (the lessee paying the other half out of his own pocket).

[11] D/DP M562–71.

reservation similar to those detailed above, was leased as a single unit from 1413, at the end of Ralph Rede's term, until 1442.

Name of Lessee	Period of Lease	Annual Rent li. s. d.	Dates of Surviving Accounts
William Chalk	6 years (1413–19)	146 13 4	1417–18
William Chalk	2 years (1419–21)	133 6 8	1421 (May to Sept. only)
Thomas Rede and John Smyth	9 years (1421–30)	140 0 0	1422–25, 1426–28
John Berdefeld, Thomas Blosine, William Bedell' and John Smyth	3 years (1431–34)	146 13 4	1431–33
Richard Josep'	3 years (1436–39)	146 13 4	1437–38
Richard Josep'	3 years (1439–42) (but only first year of term completed)	146 13 4	1439–40
Richard Algor	7 years (1440–47) (but only first 2 years completed)	146 13 4	1440–42

In general the stipulations of all the leases, as summarised in or deducible from the accounts, were similar to those contained in that granted to Ralph Rede in 1397. Particularly noticeable is an increased allowance against rent for the cost of buildings in most years especially after 1427, when the nominal annual rent was reduced by 6s. 8d. in respect of a part of the demesne taken from the lessee to form the site of a brick-field and kiln;[12] another allowance, not mentioned in Ralph Rede's account, was the continuance of the ancient payment of 4d. a day to the two (sometimes only one) monks at Bedemansberg.[13]

The account rolls do not reveal how any of the lessees worked the demesne, but analysis of the court rolls over the same period[14] suggests that the pattern of farming changed little if at all. Amercements for trespass with animals in standing crops continue as

---

[12] *Et in denar(iis) p(re)d(i)c(t)o computanti allocat(is) p(ro) firma duor(um) Campor-(um). quor(um) j vocatur le Brodefeld' (et) j voc(atur) Halfordesfeld' qui quid(e)m Campi p(er) factores de Bryke (et) comburac(i)o(n)em eor(un)d(e)m (et) vstringa ib(ide)m constructa (et) alia n(e)cc(essa)ria ad Artem suam existunt occupati . . . .vj.s' viijd'* (D/DP M570).

[13] *Et in denar(iis) solut(is) duobus Monachis presbit(er)is ordinis Clunasens(is) de domo s(an)c(t)i Joh(ann)is de Colchestre diuina celebrantib(us) in quadam Capella infra Forestum de Hiegh'wode Man(er)io de Writell' p(er)tin(entem) voc(ata) Monkesatte-bergh' vtroq(ue) capient(e) p(er) diem .ij.d'* . . . (D/DP M572).

[14] The court rolls, 1413–1447 are complete (D/DP M216–252).

hitherto; labour was provided in part if not in whole by the customary 'works' of the tenants until at least 1442,[15] when tenants were presented at courts for the last time for failure to answer summons to perform week work at harvest-time.

There appears to be some evidence that between 1413 and 1447 it was not always easy to lease the manor or for the lessee to make a success of his tenancy. When William Chalk's lease ended in 1419 there were no other takers at the same rent of 146*li.*13*s.*4*d.* and he was persuaded to continue for a further two years, on a year-to-year basis, at a rent reduced to 133*li.*6*s.*8*d.* His successors, Thomas Rede and John Smyth, in taking the manor for a term of nine years, were willing to pay additionally only half the difference between the old and the new rent paid by Chalk. In their partner-ship may be seen an attempt to share the risk, which was carried yet further in 1431 when four men joined together to farm the manor. Only in such a partnership, perhaps, was it possible to obtain the old level of rent or indeed tenants at all, for from Michaelmas 1430 to Michaelmas 1431 there was no lessee. Simi-larly there was a space of two years, between 1434 and 1436, when there was no tenant. From 1436 Richard Josep' began and completed a term of three years and was able to start a second term without any arrears on his account, but he then gave up after 12 months. The reasons for this are not apparent, for his account for that last year[16] had arrears only amounting to 17*li.*1*s.*3¼*d.* at the conclusion of the audit, which is by no means exceptional. It is, of course, possible that he lacked further money as working capital for the next year. Certainly the 1430s saw poor harvests which raised the average price of wheat in the decade to 6*s.*11*d.* a quarter.[17] Upon Josep's surrender of his lease, the farm of the manor was taken over by Richard Algor at the same annual rent of 146*li.*13*s.*4*d.*, for a seven-year term, but he too gave up manage-ment of the whole manor after two years. Unlike Josep', however, he did not disappear immediately from the scene, for he continued

---

[15] D/DP M248. By 1450 all 'works' had been sold (bailiff's account 1450–1, D/DP M575), yielding an annual income of 46*li.*11*s.*6½*d.* As late as 1523 this sum was still being accounted for as a separate item in the bailiff's account (D/DP M595), indicating that there had been no formal commutation of services.

[16] D/DP M580.

[17] In the previous decade it had been 5*s.*5*d.* and in the next it was 5*s.*4*d.*

to farm the demesne at Boyton only for two further years before giving up entirely.[18]

The restriction of the remainder of Algor's term to the Boyton demesne began a new phase in the farming of the demesne which was to last until at least 1509. Henceforth it was split into two farms which are defined in the accounts as the Manor of Writtle and the Manor of Boyton though all the manorial incidents were always assigned to the lessee of the former. The leasing of the Boyton part of the demesne was, as seen above, not new, but the period 1442–1509 is the longest recorded time when the lord's lands were continuously so divided. Again, none of the leases survives, but there are sufficient of the lessees' account rolls[19] for a reasonable survey of the period to be made.

Writtle (*i.e. southern part of the demesne*)

Name of Lessee	Period of Lease	Annual Rent			Dates of Surviving Accounts
		li.	s.	d.	
William Bedell'	7 years (1442–49)	113	6	8	1442–44, 1446–48
Henry Whitfeld	7 years (1457–64) (determined before 1460)	113	6	8	1457–58
John Bedell'	4 years (1460–64) then on an annual renewal basis, the 4-year lease still forming root of lessee's title)	113	6	8	1462–64, 1465–66, 1467–68
Alice, widow of John Bedell'	(continuation of above lease)	113	6	8	1471–72
William Forster	7 years (1473–80) (determined by 1476)	120	0	0	1473–74
Henry Pynchon	7 years (1476–83)	120	0	0	1477–78
William Lambe	9 years (1487–96)	113	6	8	1492–93
Francis Forster	(not stated)	113	6	8	1502–03
(not stated)	(not stated)	113	6	8	1508–09

Boyton (*i.e. northern part of demesne*)

Name of Lessee	Period of Lease	Annual Rent			Dates of Surviving Accounts
		li.	s.	d.	
Richard Algor	5 years (1442–47) (determined Michaelmas, 1444)	26	13	4	1443–44
Richard Stonard	7 years (1444–49)	26	13	4	1447–48

[18] It is also perhaps noteworthy that until 1436 lessees had always been found among the tenants of the manor, but neither Josep' nor Algor appear in the court rolls as having property held by manorial tenures.

[19] D/DP M571–4, 577, 581–7, 589, 592.

| Name of Lessee | Period of Lease | Annual Rent | | | Dates of Surviving |
		li.	s.	d.	Accounts
Richard Stonard	7 years (1449–56)	26	13	4	1452–53
John White	7 years (1459–65), then on an annual renewal basis until 1472	26	13	4	1462–63, 1467–68
John White	7 years (1472–79)	26	13	4	1473–74, 1477–78
(not stated)	(not stated)	26	13	4	1508–09

As the table shows, there is documentary evidence of the leasing of the 'Writtle' demesne continuously over the years 1442–1449, 1457–1472, 1472–1496, 1502–1503 and 1508–1509, and of the 'Boyton' demesne over 1442–1456, 1458–1479 and 1508–1509. Leasing may well have taken place in some of the years for which there are no lessee's accounts, but certainly from 1450 to 1455 the 'Writtle' lands were again being cultivated directly for the lord, for the accounts of the bailiff for this period are also extant.[20]

In detail both the lessees' and the bailiffs' accounts differ little from those of earlier date. As the tenants of the Boyton lands had no manorial incidents assigned to them, their accounts relate only to the annual rent and the allowances against it for repair of buildings, but those of the lessees of the Writtle lands contain all the heads of income and expenditure contained in the earlier account rolls. The one important difference in the bailiffs' accounts, 1450–1455, is the disappearance of the lengthy summary of 'works' due, performed or allowed and the appearance of a section devoted to the costs of hired agricultural labour, all 'works' having been sold for 46*li.* 11*s.* 6½*d.*

Analysis of the account rolls of the whole period under consideration shows that the relatively small area of arable under cultivation noticed in 1376–7[21] was not improved upon and, in fact, diminished still further during the 15th century. At the end of William Chalk's account for 1417–18[22] there is a statement of the acreages and crops which he had taken over at the beginning of his lease in 1413 and for which he was to answer at the end of his term:–

[20] D/DP M575–6, 578–9.
[21] See p. 69.
[22] D/DP M562.

Wheat	The crop of 156½ acres sown with 58 qrs. 5 bus., whereof in Alfaresfeld at Writtle 60 acres (whereof 20 weak) and in Great Okele at Boyton 96½ acres.
Peas	The crop of 27½ acres sown with 10 qrs. 2½ bus., whereof in Rethirwyk at Writtle 11 acres 3 roods and in Westhey at Boyton 15 acres 3 roods.
Barley	The crop of 30 acres sown with 18 qrs. 6 bus., whereof in Alfaresfeld at Writtle 9½ acres, in Bradefeld at Writtle 6½ acres and in Great Okele at Boyton 14 acres.
Drage	The crop of 22 acres sown with 13 qrs. 2 bus., whereof in Alfaresfeld at Writtle 3 acres, in Bradefeld at Writtle 14 acres and in Great Okele at Boyton 5 acres.
Pesemong	The crop of 31 acres 3 roods sown with 15 qrs. 7 bus., whereof in Rethirwyk at Writtle 7½ acres and in Westhey at Boyton 24¼ acres.
Oats	The crop of 125½ acres sown with 62 qrs. 6 bus. of oats, whereof in Rethirwyk at Writtle 38 acres, in Bradefeld at Writtle 30½ acres and in Westhey at Boyton 57 acres.

There were thus 393¼ acres under crops in 1413 when William Chalk took up his lease. From an account of his successors (referred to below), it is known that he had also to answer for 171¾ acres of fallow. No more, therefore, than 565 acres of the nearly 1,300 acres of demesne arable were under cultivation.

Unfortunately such full statements cannot be gleaned from later accounts, though a number do record the amount of fallow to be accounted for at the end of the leases. In the roll for 1431–2, the first year of the partnership of John Berdefeld, Thomas Blosine, William Bedell and John Smyth, it states that upon the election of the lady at the end of their 3-year term they were to hand back or pay a cash equivalent for 171¾ acres of fallowed land.[23] As

[23] *... remanent in man(ibus) d(i)c(t)or(um) firmar(iorum) de p(re)cio ... warectac(i)o(n)is (et) rebinacionis xxiiij acr(arum) (et) iij rodar(um) terr(e) d(omi)nice (xxxvijs'.ijd'* interlined*) ib(ide)m acra ad xiiij d' warectac(i)o(n)is rebinac(i)o(n)is (et) le Styryng' (vij.li'. iiij.s' x.d'* interlined*) lxix acr(arum) terr(e) d(omi)nice acra ad xxij.d' warectac(i)o(n)is (et) le styryng' lxxviij acr(arum) (iiijli'. iiij s. vj d'.*interlined*) t(er)re d(omi)nice acra ad xiij.d'* (D/DP M571).

mentioned above, this is said specifically to be the quantity which William Chalk answered for at the end of his lease in 1421 and presumably so did his immediate successors, Thomas Rede and John Smyth who farmed the manor from 1421 to 1431. When Richard Algor began his lease in 1440 he took over only 128 acres of fallowed land,[24] a significant drop, suggesting a total area under cultivation of less than 400 acres, or less than a third of the demesne arable.

Following the division of the demesne into two farms in 1442, the same quantities of 70 acres of fallowed land at Boyton and 58 acres at Writtle were answered for by the lessees.

Between 1450 and 1455, when the Writtle (not Boyton) lands reverted to direct cultivation for the lord under a bailiff of husbandry,[25] the acreage put under crops nearly doubled, for the figures of crops sown given below indicate about 100 acres of fallow against the 58 acres specified in the immediately preceding lease.

		Acreage Sown			
Crop	1450–1	1451–2	1452–3	1453–4	1454–5
Wheat	29	Unknown	37	40	46
Barley	46	as no	60	35	40
Oats	90½	account	60	87	89
Beans and Peas	28½	survives	27	14	38
					(peas only)
Maslin	–		4	–	–
Drage	–		–	21	6
Total	194	?	188	197	219

There is every indication that the return to direct cultivation during these years was not due to any conscious policy of reverting to the old system, but to a failure to obtain anyone willing to take a lease; the Boyton lands continued to be farmed by a tenant.

---

[24] *Et d(i)c(t)us Firmar(ius) recepit de d(i)c(t)o Comite apud Boyton' lxx acr(as) t(er)re vnde liij acr(e) warectat(e) rebinat(e) (et) striken' (et) xvij warectat(e) rebinat(e) (et) non striken' (et) apud Writell' lviij acr(as) vnde xxxiij acr(e) warectat(e) rebinat(e) (et) striken' (et) xxv warectat(e) striken' (et) non rebinat(e).* (D/DP M571).

[25] At this time the bailiff was concerned solely with income and expenditure directly concerned with agricultural operations; income from quit rents and other manorial incidents and expenditure on buildings, etc., was answered for separately on the roll by the beadle.

Moreover, despite the increase in acreage sown, the evidence points to the bailiff of husbandry merely keeping the agricultural side of the manor's economy ticking over until a new tenant was eventually found in 1457. This lies in the accounts of livestock which show that with the exception of a small number of pigs reared each year, there was no effort to breed other animals: each year the bailiff made a nil return of bulls, calves, rams, ewes and lambs. The herd of cows, around 40 in number, was let out as hitherto; small flocks of wether-sheep (between 78 and 120) were brought into the manor to be grazed, shorn and sold, but even this was not done in 1454–5.

Even the increase in the cultivated area between 1450 and 1455 was not apparently maintained in the next two years, for when a lessee for the Writtle lands was found in 1457, the fallow which he took over amounted to only 64 acres[26] and this was the quantity which all subsequent tenants answered for until 1503,[27] a tiny increase on the amount (58 acres) in 1442. At Boyton the increase was greater, 103 against 70 acres of fallowed land in 1442, at least until 1473–4, the date of the last surviving detailed account.[28]

For more than a century and a quarter then, by far the greater part of the demesne arable grew no crops. The possibility that this was due to conversion to pasture for sheep-rearing on a much larger scale than before receives no support from the evidence of the account rolls or the court rolls. It is, therefore, necessary to consider whether Writtle provides a further illustration of that contraction of the economy in Britain as in the rest of Europe during the later medieval period, coupled with a decline in population.[29]

---

[26] Account roll, 1457–58 (D/DP M583).
[27] Account roll, 1502–03 (D/DP M592).
[28] Account roll, 1473–74 (D/DP M589).
[29] While there is now wide agreement among historians that this was generally so, the reasons for it remain still a matter for argument. The most notable work on the subject in this country has been done by Professor M. M. Postan in such articles as 'Some Economic Evidence of Declining Population in the Later Middle Ages', *Economic History Review*, 2nd series, vol. ii (1950), pp. 221–41, and (with J. Titow) 'Heriots and Prices on Winchester Manors', *ibid.*, 2nd series, vol. xi (1958–59), pp. 392–410, also 'Note', *ibid.*, 2nd series, vol. xii (1959–60), pp. 72–82. Adopting a Malthusian approach he considers that the rapid growth of population in the 12th and 13th centuries led to the cultivation of a good deal of inferior land which in time became exhausted. While plenty of land remained available, even of

(continued overleaf)

While there is no direct evidence one way or the other that any of the demesne arable at Writtle suffered from soil exhaustion in the 14th century, it would seem highly unlikely, given the known quality of the soil. Moreover, had it been so, one would have expected to have found the small acreage under cultivation in the last quarter of the 14th century and throughout the 15th century being moved about over the whole extent of the demesne arable. Accepting, however, that this factor was widely at work elsewhere, and that population was generally declining, at times sharply throughout the country, it follows that land at Writtle would in due course of time fall out of cultivation as demand slackened.

If the manorial records of Writtle offer no positive illustration of the theory of soil exhaustion, they do yield valuable evidence of the population trend in the manor during the 14th and 15th centuries and in a way not generally possible. Normally population studies based on manorial records are based on counting the number of households given in surveys and extents and applying a 'multiplier' to estimate the whole population. A good deal of work has been done in this way, but the lack of agreement on what constitutes a reliable 'multiplier', particularly in the 14th century, a period of wide fluctuations, reduces considerably confidence in the results of such investigations.[30]

In the case of Writtle, this approach is, in fact, not possible, for the only detailed extent in the whole of the 14th and 15th centuries is that made in 1328,[31] which relates to only two thirds of the manor, and any tally of households would inevitably be incomplete for one tenant is said to hold 'tenements in the vill of Writtle' which could account for any number of dwellings.

The Extent of 1328, however, and the court rolls from 1382 to

---

marginal quality, this did not matter, since agriculture could be carried on extensively, if not intensively, but once such extensions of the cultivated areas became impossible or limited, there followed inevitably a decline in productivity, which coupled with famine and plague, brought a long, continuous rise in the death rate and thus a long continuous decline in population. Such a situation had arisen in England by about 1300.

[30] Compare, for example, J. C. Russell, *British Medieval Population* (Albuquerque, 1948), G. C. Homans, *English Villagers in the Thirteenth Century* (Cambridge, Mass., 1941), and J. Krause, 'The Medieval Household: Large or Small?', *Economic History Review*, 2nd series, vol. x (1957), pp. 420–32.

[31] D/DP M540.

1492[32] do provide one set of population statistics which may be used with some confidence, if caution is not wholly abandoned. The basis of the figures is the common fine which was uncertain, being paid at a rate of ½d. a head by all males over the age of twelve years in tithing who owed attendance at the view of frank-pledge held annually on Whitsun Monday. By converting the total sum received into halfpennies the total of decenners, including chief pledges, who contributed is arrived at. This number does not represent the total male population over the age of 12, for it is clear that only those who actually attended the view paid; but where the numbers of chief pledges making default, decenners bailed by their chief pledges for appearance at the next court, men and lads who came to be sworn into tithing for the first time and those presented for not coming to be sworn, can be discovered and are added, a figure not far removed from an absolute total is found. It is recognised that there must always have been those who managed to escape the net and who were not included in any of the above categories. But there is no reason to believe that this number was ever high, for the totals of absentees presented are usually sufficiently high to infer that the chief pledges exercised a tight control in their 'quarters' of the manor.[33]

The value of the common fine in 1328 given in the Extent is 17s.,[34] equivalent to 408 polls. Since the Extent relates to two thirds of the manor a total of 612 for the whole lordship is to be implied. It is not wholly clear whether the sum of 17s. represents the amount due if all on the then current list of decenners attended the next view or the sum actually collected at the last. If the latter, then the total number of decenners was no doubt higher, allowing for all absentees; but the former is more likely, as values

---

[32] D/DP M189–296.

[33] E.g.

	1387	1403
Decenners present at view	232	202
Decenners bailed by chief pledges	34	46
Decenners making default	5	15
Those newly sworn into tithing	5	1
Those amerced for being out of tithing	3	8
Total	279	272

[34] *Et est ib(ide)m qued(am) cons(uetudino) d(i)c(t)o die vis(us) q(uo)d quil(ibe)t qui debet advent(um) ad eund(em) debit p(ro) cap(ite) suo ob(olum) et valet illa cons-(uetudino) hoc a(nn)o xvijs'.*

in extents usually represent sums calculated without regard for exceptions, allowances or excuses.

Unfortunately there is no basis for comparison before 1328 and none thereafter until 1382; from then, however, figures for a significant number of years can be compiled as outlined above.

Year	Recorded no. of males aged 12 or over	Year	Recorded no. of males aged 12 or over
1382	268	1454	239
1383	258	1457	207
1387	279	1459	221
1388	273	1460	234
1391	269	1461	222
1392	258	1462	216
1393	269	1463	214
1394	276	1464	213
1400	247	1465	225
1403	272	1466	224
1404	255	1467	224
1407	219	1468	215
1410	215	1469	219
1411	192	1470	239
1412	193	1471	222
1413	207	1472	223
1414	215	1474	213
1416	207	1476	218
1417	203	1478	221
1419	202	1489	208
1440	185[35]	1491	239[36]
1446	211	1492	277

It is impossible to say with complete accuracy what proportion of the whole population these figures represent, for there is no record of male children under the age of twelve or of females of any age; and even if the validity of the life tables and other statistical tests devised by Professor Russell are acceptable[37] over a wide range of population, it would be dangerous to apply them

[35] Total taken from decenners' list (D/DP M245).
[36] Total taken from decenners' list (D/DP M295).
[37] I. C. Russell, *op. cit.;* J. Krause, *op. cit.,* pp. 426–30.

to a single community which is not necessarily typical. At best it may be hazarded that doubling any of the figures would give the approximate number of males and females aged twelve years or over, and that the addition of one third of this total (to represent those under 12 years) would give the overall population;[38] but the proportion of men to women and of children under twelve to persons of twelve and over may well have fluctuated widely from decade to decade, particularly in an unstable era.

Setting aside, however, the significance of the figures in absolute terms, there is no doubt that used relatively they indicate a very heavy drop in population between 1328 and 1382. Whether the Black Death played any part in this must be deduced. That it reached the borders of the manor is evidenced in a petition by Thomas Hughe, undated but *c.*1377,[39] to 'la countesse de Hereforde', concerning the disseisin of property in Moulsham made with the assistance of 'Raude Reede votre Bailif' de Writelle', which makes reference to 'la primere pestilence'. The use of the word 'primere' indicates that one or more of the further outbreaks of plague in 1361–1368 (*pestis secunda*), 1368–1369 and 1375 spread to the neighbourhood. The court rolls of the Manor of Fingrith Hall in Blackmore on the western border of Writtle record in stark, factual detail how the first outbreak eliminated between 85 and 90 per cent. of the landholders.[40] Indeed the percentage fall (56.86) in the number of decenners at Writtle between 1328 and 1382 in itself implies the influence of such catastrophe. There is further confirmation when the genealogical evidence is also considered, for out of 126 family names in the Extent of 1328 70 do not occur in the court rolls from 1379 to 1502, a loss of 55.6 per cent. of names.

The only other figure of population in Writtle in the 14th century is to be found by simple arithmetic in the receipt for the poll

---

[38] i.e., the suggested 'multiplier' is $2\frac{2}{3}(2.67)$. For an example of its application see p. 82.

[39] Preserved among the muniments of Wadham College, Oxford. Transcribed by C. R. Cheney in 'Medieval Charters relating to the Manor of Mountpillers, Writtle, Essex', pp. 245–6. Typescript copy in Essex Record Office (T/A 139). Ralph Rede was Bailiff in 1376–7 (D/DP M560).

[40] D/DK M1. For analysis of the court rolls see microfilm record of Essex Record Office Exhibition, 1962, 'Essex in the Middle Ages'.

tax of 1377, which gives a total of 600 polls.[41]   It is difficult to use this, however, as a basis of comparison with the total of 268 decenners in 1382. Firstly, the poll tax was based on persons, male and female, aged over 15 years of age, not 12 years; it took in not only those resident in the Manor of Writtle but also those, no doubt small in number, who were within the jurisdiction of the Manors of Romans Fee and Newland Hall;[42]   the extent of exemptions and evasions from the tax in 1377 is uncertain and therefore in dispute;[43]   and lastly there is a gap of five years between the two figures. Even so, allowing for all these unknown quantities, an estimated total population of the Manor of Writtle of 716 arrived at by applying the suggested 'multiplier' of 2.67 would appear to be proportionately not unreasonable.

The numbers recorded in the above list for the years after 1382 indicate that the population of the manor remained fairly stable until the first years of the 15th century and then suffered a further significant decline between 1404 and 1411. After this date there are few marked fluctuations throughout much of the rest of the century until the steep rise in the figures for 1491 and 1492.[44]

If the general fall in the population of the country was anywhere near that which demonstrably took place in Writtle, the amount of demesne arable which fell and remained derelict is explicable.[45]

Most surprisingly, however, the dramatic decline in both population and productivity of the demesne is not paralleled by a marked increase in the number of holdings without occupants. In the bailiffs' accounts, 1360–1 and 1376–7, under *'Defectus*

---

[41]   P.R.O., E.179/107/46. Only the receipt is extant for 1377 and no returns at all for 1379 or 1381.

[42]   See p. 37.

[43]   J. C. Russell, *op. cit.,* pp. 26–30; J. Krause, *op. cit.,* p. 425.

[44]   Since the lowest recorded figure, 185 in 1440, and one of the later higher figures, 239 in 1491, derive from decenners' lists it cannot be argued that the lists show that the calculated figures for other years are significantly under-estimates.

[45]   Professor Russell (*op. cit.*) estimates that between 1348 and 1377 the population of England fell from 3,700,000 to 2,232,373 or almost 40 per cent., compared with 56.86 per cent. at Writtle between 1328 and 1382, reckoned above. Given the longer date range in the case of the Writtle estimate the two percentages are in no way incompatible, if it is accepted that the decline began around 1300 (see p. 77 above). For an example of a community, where population and trade increased very considerably between 1348 and 1400, see my *Thaxted in the Fourteenth Century,* pp. 26–7.

reddituum´, only 3 tenements (not further described), with rents totalling but 2*s*.6*d*. and a shop in the market place are recorded as being in the lord's hands. The court rolls and accounts of later date offer no evidence that this small number of unimportant tenants' holdings was significantly added to. The conclusion must be drawn that in 1328 there was a very large element in the population made up either of the landless or of those who were able to rent acres from the tenants of the manor. The former, no doubt, suffered particularly from the outbreaks of plague, but some of them and sufficient of the latter survived to enter into the manorial holdings of families that were wiped out.

It might have been thought that high population before 1328 would have led to fragmentation of holdings, even in a manor where primogeniture was the rule not only where there were sons, but also in families with all daughters, as demand upon available land increased. But as the tables of holdings in Chapter IV show, there was relatively little by 1328. When the court rolls from 1379 to 1500 are analysed, however, fragmentation is found to accompany decline of population.

Size of Holding	Total identified in court rolls 1379–1500	No. still unfrag- mented	No. found frag- mented under no. of fragments identified								Total of fragmented holdings
			2	3	4	5	6	7	8	9	
Virgate	17	3	4	2	–	3	1	1	1	2	14
¾ virg.	1	1	–	–	–	–	–	–	–	–	–
½ virg.	29	7	9	6	1	2	1	1	1	1	22
⅓ virg.	18½	3½	9	2	2	2	–	–	–	–	15
¼ virg.	16	4	9	3	–	–	–	–	–	–	12

The figures in the Table are not exhaustive, for in the case of certain holdings the number of fragments identified by no means adds up to the total acreage, some, no doubt, having lost the name of the holding to which they had originally belonged. In these instances the degree of fragmentation is understated. Nevertheless the figures are sufficient to support the contention made.

To illustrate this by specific examples, the break-up of two holdings, a virgate called 'Wolvynesyerde' and a ⅓-virgate named 'Levesonnysforman', may be traced through the court rolls. In 1328 Richard Wolvyne held a messuage and undivided virgate of land. Before 1391 it had been divided into four parts, the bulk of it, three quarters or nominally 60 acres, being held by Nicholas Rochell,[46] 1 acre by Richard Johann, 8 acres by John Herry and the messuage and 10 acres by John Broun.[47] By 1392 Nicholas Rochell had sold off the greater part of his land, for he is recorded as then holding only 14 acres of land and 1 acre of meadow[48] and in 1419 when it was purchased by John Crane, Rochell's parcel of the virgate was stated to contain 12 acres.[49] Further fragments— 5, 12, 12 and 2 acres of land and 1 acre of meadow—of Rochell's three quarters of the virgate are found in the court rolls by 1446, all in the hands of different tenants.[50] The ⅓ virgate held undivided by William Levesone in 1328 split into parcels of 1, 3, 3½, 4 and 9 acres, each in the hands of a different person certainly by 1467.[51]

In both cases, the family of the holder in 1328 no longer had any interest in any part of the holding and their names are indeed no longer to be found in the court rolls, 1379–1500. But a not dissimilar process of fragmentation could occur when the descendants of a tenant of an undivided holding in 1328 retained an interest in some part of the property. John Guch had held a messuage and undivided virgate of land in 1328. Before 1378 three quarters of the land had been acquired by John Rote, from whom in that year it was acquired by Richard, clerk of William Skreyne,[52] possibly on behalf of his master, for it was in the possession of that family in 1445,[53] but the greater part of the remainder (at least 17½ acres) was still in the hands of a Guch, another John, between 1416 and 1422,[54] while a Walter Guch held a piece of meadow

[46] D/DP M192.
[47] D/DP M197.
[48] *Ibid.*
[49] D/DP M224. Rochell was one of the bigger landholders, his diminishing share in this virgate being only part of his possessions (see p. 90).
[50] D/DP M203, 223–4, 248–9.
[51] D/DP M219, 222–4, 249, 269.
[52] D/DP M201.
[53] D/DP M249.
[54] D/DP M220, 226.

which had belonged to the virgate.[55]   The three quarters of the holding remained intact, because it became merged in the large estate of the Skreen family, throughout the 15th century, but by 1467 only a messuage and 5 acres were in the possession of a member of the Guch family,[56] while fragments of 1, 3, 4 and 4 acres had passed into the hands of others.[57]

Thus, fragmentation of holdings, which is seen to have accompanied a heavy fall in population, did not necessarily depend on plague or other factors totally eliminating families which had originally possessed them.

---

[55] D/DP M195.
[56] D/DP M226.
[57] D/DP M200, 203, 262, 265. The two parcels of four acres are not one and the same, for they are shown to be in the hands of different manorial tenants at the same court.

VII

THE STABILISING FORCE

With the breakdown of its old economic structure there is often a tendency to write off the manor as an institution of importance. This is to ignore its functions as the only organ of civil justice and administration at the lowest level—the local community. Not until the time of the Tudors were functions of local government imposed upon the parish which hitherto had been concerned only with ecclesiastical affairs.[1] But in this process the Tudor legislators were by no means unaware of the existing manorial organisation. By the Statute of Bridges, 1530 (22 Hen. VIII, *cap.* 5), the justices of the peace were empowered to tax the inhabitants with the assent of the constables (who were appointed usually at the court leet), or two other inhabitants in their absence, for the repair of bridges where the legal liability to do so of any 'persons, lands, tenements or body politic' could not be proved. Under the Statute for Mending of Highways, 1555 (2 & 3 Phil. & Mary, *cap.* 8), it was not only enacted that the constables and churchwardens were to arrange for the election of the parish surveyors, but 'the steward and stewards of every leet or law-day shall therein have full power and authority to enquire by the oaths of the suitors, of all and every the offences that shall be committed within the leet or law-day, against every point and article of this estatute, and to assess such reasonable fines and amercements for the same, as shall be meet by the said steward'; and the steward had further to 'make estreats indented of all the fines, forfeitures and amercements for the defaults presented before him, and (to) deliver the one part thereof sealed and signed by him to the bailiff and high constable of every hundred, rape, lathe or wapentake, wherein the defaults shall be presented'. Although reserve powers were given to the justices of the peace to act in default of the steward of a leet, the implementation of the

---

[1] In those communities where there is evidence of non-manorial village assemblies (Writtle is not one of these), there is no reason to believe that the parish was necessarily the unit. For examples of such assemblies, see W. O. Ault, 'Village Assemblies in Medieval England', *Studies presented in the International Commission for the History of Representative and Parliamentary Institutions*, vol. xxiii (Louvain U.P., 1960), pp. 9–35.

Act by the usual method of presentment and the imposition of pains and penalties upon defaulters was squarely placed upon the existing manorial jurisdiction.[2] The penal laws directed against the poor dealing with hedgebreaking, stealing of wood, the taking in of 'inmates' were also implemented, often vigorously, through the courts leet, particularly in the reign of Elizabeth I. Indeed the spate of such legislation under the Tudors acted as a rejuvenating agent on such courts, especially in the more populous manors, which lasted in at least some cases well into the 17th century.[3]

Of no manor was all this more true than of Writtle. With its wider jurisdiction as a manor in ancient demesne[4] and large population, the holding of a court from three weeks to three weeks was nearly and sometimes wholly a reality in the last quarter of the 14th century for which there are court rolls and throughout the 15th and 16th centuries.[5]

The use of the little writ of right meant that all stages in the process of pleas of land were conducted in the manor court[6] and all rolls contain records of them with the writ sewn to the margin; in the later rolls the recoveries suffered and fines levied are registered in full.[7] There was no limit on the amount involved in pleas of debt as in the case of manors not in ancient demesne where it was fixed at under 40 shillings.[8] Any attempt by anyone, tenant or outsider, to implead a tenant in any court outside the manor was deemed a serious 'injury' to the liberties and franchises of the

---

[2] After the passing of the Highways Act, the first surveyors of the highways for Writtle were appointed at the court leet held on Whitsun Monday, 1556 (D/DP M325). And thereafter presentments of ways out of repair and orders for their maintenance were frequently made until 1769 (D/DP M418).

[3] See unpublished abstracts of the court rolls of a number of Essex manors in the Elizabethan period, prepared by myself, in the Essex Record Office.

[4] See p. 13, n. 72.

[5] Thus in 13 years of the reign of Richard II for which there are annual rolls an average of 10.3 courts annually were held; in 21 years of the reign of Edward IV the average was 8.66 courts and in 41 years of the reign of Elizabeth I 8.24 courts.

[6] The jurisdiction of manors not in ancient demesne in relation to pleas of freehold land extended only up to the point where the action was removed to the king's court for the grand assize; though in time they developed a procedure similar to that obtaining on ancient demesne for dealing with copyholds.

[7] The last little writ of right to be returned in the Manor of Writtle was at a court held on 5 October 1833 shortly before the passing of the Act abolishing Fines and Recoveries (3 & 4 Wm. IV, *cap.* 74).

[8] The largest sum involved in a plea of debt found in the court rolls was £140 (Court held 8 December 1543, D/DP M314).

lordship and to the damage of the tenant. When John Bysshopp',
a tenant of Writtle, impleaded John Saveryn, another tenant, in
the court of the Hundred of Chelmsford in 1443, he was amerced
12*d.* for having done so.[9]   Similarly, in 1423, Thomas Ruddok
was amerced 6*s.* 8*d.* for having unlawfully vexed John Bysshop'
(?the same as the above) at common law by a royal writ of *de
recordare* and William Trot was similarly dealt with for the like
offence against John Esthey.[10]   A late declaration of custom
(1547) deemed that the levying of a fine at common law 'reduced'
the property involved to ancient demesne (i.e. it escheated to the
lord).[11] This case is of particular interest, for the estate involved
was the submanor of Mountneys, one of the so-called 'free' holdings, in the Extent of 1328.[12]   Fortunately for the owner of
Mountneys his offence was pardoned.

In relation to civil pleas the Manor of Writtle was in effect an
exempt jurisdiction, scarcely touched by the Hundred Court or
indeed by the central courts. Meetings of its court involved the
appearance of professional lawyers just as in the royal courts in
London.[13]   This becomes apparent, however, only when there is a
dispute about their payment.

This exclusiveness of jurisdiction in the matter of civil actions
was paralleled in large degree in the execution of the criminal law.
Attempts to indict tenants of the manor before the *justicarii ad
pacem* for the county brought in its train amercements, on
occasion heavy, for those committing this infringement of the
jurisdiction of the lordship. In 1450 Thomas atte Lee of Beadles
End in Writtle 'with other persons well disposed towards him
maliciously indicted' John Chopyn and three other tenants 'before

---

[9] D/DP M248.
[10] D/DP M227.
[11] D/DP M317.
[12] See pp. 42–3 above.
[13] For example, in 1388 John Fech' entered a plea of debt against Roger Bolyn,
alleging that the defendant owed him 26*s.* 8*d.* for certain land sold to him by the
plaintiff, 6*s.* 8*d.* for (the fee for) an assize of fresh force in the manor court and
6*s.* 7¾*d.* for the fee of Roger Germeyn, *hominis ad legem* (D/DP M194). This is dis-
proof of the view that 'all foreign elements in the shape of advocates or professional
pleaders were excluded from the manor court' advanced by P. Vinogradoff (*Villain-
age in England* (1891), p. 367), at least as far as ancient demesne manors are concerned. See also H. S. Bennett, *Life on the English Manor,* p. 221, though the illustration he gives is ill chosen, for *per attornatum suum* does not necessarily imply a
professional advocate (*cf.* letters of attorney).

the Justices of the Lord King for the Peace in their Sessions at Chelmsford to their damage not a little and in injury of the liberty and franchise of the lordship'.[14] And in 1523 Thomas Combys and Richard Bedyll, gentlemen, were each fined £5 for procuring the indictment of a number of tenants at the Sessions of the Peace at Chelmsford 'against the ordinance and custom of the manor before this time and the time of which the mind of man is not to the contrary, to the pernicious example of other inhabitants'.[15] Yet a further case, in 1482, makes it quite clear that the manor's jurisdiction extended to felony,[16] though there is no record of any attempt to deal with a case of murder even in the first instance. Indeed it would seem that any serious cases of felony were sent to be tried by the King's justices. For example, in 1473 Thomas Lawkyn was arrested in the manor for felony and was removed to Colchester Gaol. No attempt was made to deal with his unspecified crimes in the manor court, but clearly the right to arrest him and to decide whether he should be sent out of the manor for trial was implicitly asserted on behalf of the lord.[17]

Despite this wider jurisdiction, indeed, the catalogue of offences which can be compiled from the rolls recording the annual meeting of the view of frankpledge and court leet on Whitsun Monday differs hardly from that which could be extracted from the rolls of any one of hundreds of manors with a leet. The frequency of offences appears high but not when related to the size of the manor in population and extent, which necessitated the appointment of four constables to maintain the king's peace,[18] two for Writtle *infra barras* and two for *Rokeswell et alibi in villata de Wretell extra barras*.[19] It would appear that they were elected by the chief pledges of the areas of the manor in which they carried

---

[14] D/DP M255.

[15] D/DP M302.

[16] 'It is presented by all the chief pledges that John Brette laboured to indict John Bute, John Poway and Robert Fuller, whereby they were indicted of felony before the Justices for the Peace in the county of Essex, without this liberty, against the custom of this manor in grave contempt of the lord'. Brette was amerced 3s.4d. (D/DP M286).

[17] Court roll, 1473 (D/DP M276).

[18] The Manors of Romans Fee and Newland Hall each had two constables, at least in the 16th century, so that there were probably eight in all exercising office within the bounds of the parish.

[19] Court roll, 1432–1433 (D/DP M239).

out their duties,[20] but their election is not recorded on the rolls until the beginning of the reign of Henry VI.[21]   As the chief pledges also elected others to vacancies within their own ranks,[22] the day-to-day maintenance of law and order was in the hands of a small band of men who were in effect a self-perpetuating oligarchy.   Analysis of the court rolls shows that the constables were drawn from the better-off landholders.   To take but one example, Nicholas Rochell who held the office from 1441 to 1443[23] possessed one of the few undivided virgates still remaining at that time,[24] a (diminishing) part of Wolvynesyerde[25] and a tenement and two fields.[26]   Quite a number of farms in Writtle today bear the family names of those who served in the office of constable in the 15th century.

The protection of the consumer in the purchase of the staple commodities of ale and bread was in the hands of six aletasters who served their office in pairs in the three areas of Writtle, Highwood and Roxwell into which the manor was territorially divided for this purpose.   Although more than 30 brewers and regrators of ale[27] and up to 7 bakers[28] might be presented for breaking the assize at any one of the three courts held yearly for taking the assize, the monotonous regularity with which the same names occur at court after court compels the conclusion that the amercements varying from 1*d.* to 1*s.* were regarded by the offenders as payment for licence to continue as before; and the two or three butchers who sold meat too dearly,[29] the one or two candlemakers who overcharged or sold guttering candles 'in deception of the people'[30] and tanners who sold badly tanned leather at excessive

---

[20] Court roll, 1431–1432 (D/DP M238).

[21] Court roll, 1422–1423 (D/DP M227).

[22] Court rolls, 1472–1473 and 1474 (D/DP M275, 278).

[23] Court rolls, 1430–1431 and 1431–1432 (D/DP M234, 238).

[24] Court roll, 1441–1442 (D/DP M247).

[25] See p. 84.

[26] Court roll, 1431–1432 (D/DP M238).

[27] Court roll, 1381–1382 (D/DP M189). Forfeiture of ale by the brewers occurs seldom.

[28] Court roll, 1462–1463 (D/DP M265).

[29] Butchers dwelling *extra burgum* had also to pay annually a ploughshare worth 16*d.* *Burgus* is used here and elsewhere in the court rolls only as the equivalent of *forum* or *mercatum* which are also occasionally used in the same contexts (e.g. court rolls, 1381–1382 and 1402–1403. D/DP M189, 206).

[30] Candlemakers are not found as offenders in the rolls until the 1440s.

prices, the two millers who used unsealed measures, each of whom could no doubt 'stelen corn and tollen thryes'[31] and even the odd tailor who misused his craft[32] were apparently of like mind.

If the nature of the offences and 'nuisances' found in the Writtle rolls is generally little different from those found in the rolls of other manors, one—incontinency—is conspicuous by its almost total absence in the years 1379 to 1500, except for one brief period which will be mentioned below. H. S. Bennett has drawn attention to the prevalence of this offence as an item of court business[33] and F. W. Maitland gives a number of examples culled from early rolls of a number of manors.[34]   Similarly, although it was the custom of the Manor of Writtle that either the mother or the father of an illegitimate child was amerced 3s. 4d. for a 'child-wite', there is only one instance of its being exacted before 1555.[35] Since it is unlikely that human nature differed so greatly in Writtle, the lack of incidence of immorality in the rolls is to be seen as a good illustration that the tenant in ancient demesne or members of his family were not chattels of the lord, who was not therefore concerned with the depreciation of their value as a result of such acts, but left punishment to the ecclesiastical authorities.

Yet the undoubted jurisdiction of the manor court at Writtle over the offence could be directed against a particular class of person—the clergy.   There is the sudden appearance in the rolls of presentments of clergy and those of the laity involved with them for immorality in 1431 which ends in 1433 as suddenly as it had begun.[36]   Since the low state of morality among the priesthood was obviously not confined to so short a space of time and is indeed well documented over a much longer period,[37] one may

---

[31] e.g. Court roll, 1381–1382 (D/DP M238).

[32] Court roll, 1382–1383 (D/DP M190).

[33] H. S. Bennett, *Life on the English Manor,* pp. 246–8.

[34] *Select Pleas in Manorial and Other Seignorial Courts* (Selden Society, vol. ii, 1889), pp. 1, 12, 29, 92, 97, 98, 162.

[35] Court roll, 1411–1412 (D/DP M215).

[36] In 1397, John Markyn had been amerced 6s. 8d. for knowingly harbouring Agnes, concubine of Thomas Bowyere, chaplain, and Christine, wife of William Peion, concubine of the parochial chaplain (unnamed) of Writtle, but no action was taken against the priests or the women. (D/DP M200).

[37] e.g. The Hereford Visitation, 1397. See H. S. Bennett, *op. cit.,* pp. 332ff.; see also G. C. Coulton, *Old England,* Chapter XVI, and *English Historical Review,* xliv, pp. 279–89, 444–53, xlv, pp. 444–63.

see in these presentments one of the outbreaks of anticlericalism of the period rather than a sudden concern for the moral welfare of society.

That this was so is perhaps illustrated by the first of the presentments in 1431, which accused Alice Lokewayte of being a common whore and procuress of divers priests and *other felons* by day and night.[38] Even if the use of the words 'other felons' was in fact a clerical slip, it is none the less revealing of an attitude of mind. At the same court Robert the chaplain celebrating masses for the soul of Giles Rede in Writtle church was amerced the large sum of 33*s.* 4*d.* for ravishing Christine, wife of William Kendale, before the Feast of the Purification of the Blessed Virgin Mary, 9 Henry VI (2 February 1430/1), and for continuing to do so until the day of the court (21 May 1431); and Thomas Furnour, the vicar, was amerced 20*s.* for approvingly giving support to Robert, knowing that he had committed the ravishing, and for requesting John Wyse, a chief pledge, not to declare the misdeeds of Alice Lokewayte. In the next year John Syger of Oxney Green was presented for harbouring Joan, formerly servant of John Sprotte of 'Badewe' (Great or Little Baddow), knowing that she would be ravished and sullied by Nicholas clerk of the chapel of 'Badewe' and was threatened with a heavy amercement of 20*s.* if he did not get rid of her.[39] In 1433 John Brayles, a chaplain, was amerced 26*s.* 8*d.* for entering the close and house of the same Alice Lokewayte and ravishing her.

There is some further evidence that these presentments were all part of a general resentment against the priesthood at this time which led to any offence, not only those against morality, by the clergy being seized upon. In 1426 Nicholas, parochial chaplain of Roxwell, was accused of refusing unlawfully and without due process of law to minister the sacrament to John Laur' from Easter Sunday to the following Thursday, because John owed William Parker two bushels of corn 'to the grave scandal of John and the great disgust of all his neighbours'. The matter was referred to the lady's council and the result of their deliberations is unknown.[40] At the same court as Robert the chaplain and the vicar were

---

[38] Court roll, 1430–1431 (D/DP M234).
[39] Court roll, 1431–1432 (D/DP M238).
[40] Court roll, 1425–1426 (D/DP M230).

presented for their offences against morality, it was reported that Thomas, the former chaplain of Roxwell was arrested there upon suspicion of plundering the rectory of 'Hanefeld' (East, West or South Hanningfield) and had been put in the stocks. He managed, however, to escape to the church where he took sanctuary for 14 days before making good his escape. For this the two constables were blamed and they and the whole vill were ordered to give satisfaction at the next court for the escape.[41] In 1434 the same vicar was further accused of putting his horse in the graveyard, sometimes tethering it by ropes to graves, so that it knocked down the crosses by encircling them and rubbing itself against them as well as fouling not only the ways and paths but also the porches and holy water there 'to the great opprobrium and violation of the country, contrary to the warnings of the parish and against the king's peace.'[42]

To give some balance to this picture of an immoral, felonious and irresponsible clergy, it is possible that priests of the calibre of Chaucer's 'poure parson' were not entirely unknown in Writtle, for when John Loksmyth *alias* Fynchyngfeld procured a jury to indict Alexander Halton, a chaplain, for various unspecified felonies his action was described as 'malevolent and to the great scandal of Alexander'; but as it was also an infringement of the jurisdiction of the manor, this may have been the principal reason for the presentment.[43]

These few examples illustrate what every court roll of the Manor of Writtle evidences throughout the 15th century—and indeed the 16th century—that the break-up of the old economic structure of the manor did not lead to a decline in its functions as an organ of local justice and administration, nor had these functions become so petrified that they were unable to reflect the state and attitudes of the community. 'Dilatory, capricious and uncertain'[44] its courts no doubt were, but such an assessment could be more strongly applied to the central royal courts and not only in that age. In fact no adequate alternatives to the jurisdiction of the manor at local level had been devised or had evolved by the

[41] Court roll, 1430–1431 (D/DP M234).
[42] Court roll, 1433–1434 (D/DP M240).
[43] Court roll, 1425–1426 (D/DP M230).
[44] Bennett, *op. cit.,* p. 220.

end of the 15th century; and in accordance with the lawyer's dictum that justice is great profit, it was in the interests of lords particularly of populous manors in ancient demesne with wide jurisdiction in civil pleas and criminal matters that their courts should not decline. It is no less true that it was also in the interests of the inhabitants that this should be so: resort to the manor court was cheaper[45] and the affairs of the community were kept within its own bounds free from the verdicts and interference of out-siders. The firm impression of an inward-looking community, which had its roots in the period when Writtle ceased to be of importance as the centre of the Hundred and the County, was much encouraged and supported by these considerations.

---

[45] For example, the fee for a recovery or fine of lands was only 6*s.* 8*d.* from the 14th to the 19th century.

APPENDICES

APPENDIX 'A'

DOMESDAY STATISTICS OF WRITTLE

	T.R.E.		1086	
Hidage	Hides	Acres	Hides	Acres
Manor of Writtle	16		14	
Lands of Count Eustace Newlanda (Newland Hall in Roxwell)[1]	–		2	
Formerly of a sokeman	½		½	
Lands of the Bishop of Hereford				
Formerly of a priest	1		1	
Formerly belonging to the church	1	20	1	20
Land held by 2 sokemen	½	10	½	10
Total	19	30	19	30

[1] This is the figure given in the main Writtle entry (D.B.ii, f. 5b); under the lands of Count Eustace (f. 31) it is entered as 3 hides and with a different valuation. For a discussion of this, see p. 5.

APPENDIX 'A' *(Continued)*

		T.R.E.		1086	
Tenants					
Villeins	⎫	97		73	
Bordars		36		60	
Serfs	Manor of Writtle	24		18	
Swineherd		1		–	
Sokemen	⎭	3		2	
	Total	161	161	153	153
Villeins	⎫	15		15	
Bordars	Newlanda	7		7	
Serfs	⎭	2		2	
	Total	24	24	24	24
Villeins	⎫	3		3	
Bordars	Lands of Bishop	2		8	
Serfs	of Hereford	2		–	
Priests	⎭	2		1	
	Total	9	9	12	12
	Sum Totals		194		189

Ploughs		T.R.E.	1086
Demesne	⎫ Manor of Writtle	12	9
Men	⎭	64	45
Demesne	⎫ Newlanda	2	2
Men	⎭	2	2
Demesne	⎫ Lands of Bishop	1	1
Men	⎭ of Hereford	2	2
Two sokemen		½	½
	Total	83½	61½

APPENDIX 'A' *(Continued)*

		T.R.E.	1086
Woodland (for swine)			
Manor of Writtle		1,500	1,200
Newlanda		100?	100
Bishop of Hereford		100?	100
	Total	1,700?	1,400
Meadow			
Manor of Writtle		?	80 acres
Newlanda		?	20 acres
Bishop of Hereford		?	8 acres
Two sokemen		?	4 acres
	Total	?	112 acres
Mills			
Manor of Writtle		1	2
Livestock			
Rounceys		9	9
Colts		5	5
Beasts		40	40
Sheep		318	318
Swine		172	172
Values			
Manor of Writtle (incl. the two sokemen)		£10 & 10 nights' feorm	£100 & 100s. (for lease)
Newlanda		100s.	£7 (£12 in main entry)
Lands of Bishop of Hereford		–	50s.

APPENDIX 'B'

POPULATION STATISTICS OF CHELMSFORD HUNDRED RECORDED IN THE LITTLE DOMESDAY BOOK

		Villains	Bordars	Serfs	Freemen (F) or Sokemen (S)	Others	Totals	Sum Totals T.R.E.	Sum Totals 1086
Writtle	T.R.E.	97	36	24	3 (S)	1 swineherd	161	194	
	1086	73	60	18	2 (S)	–	153		189
Newlanda (in Roxwell in *Writtle*)	T.R.E.	15	7	2	–	–	26		
	1086	15	7	2	–	–	24		
Lands of Bishop of Hereford in *Writtle*	T.R.E.	3	2	2	–	2 priests	9		
	1086	3	8	–	–	1 priest	12		
Baddow, Great (*a*)	T.R.E.	16	8	6	–	–	30	35	
	1086	16	15	6	3 (S)	–	40		47
Baddow, Great (*b*)	T.R.E.	–	1	4	–	–	5		
	1086	–	3	4	–	–	7		
Baddow, Little (*a*)	T.R.E.	3	4	6	–	–	13	31	
	1086	–	8	3	–	–	11		27
Baddow, Little (*b*)	T.R.E.	2	2	9	5 (F)	–	18		
	1086	2	2	7	5 (F)	–	16		
Blackmore	T.R.E.	6	8	–	–	–	14	14	
	1086	6	8	–	–	–	14		14
Boreham (*a*)	T.R.E.	–	4	3	14 (F)	–	21		
	1086	–	8	3	1 (F)	–	12		

APPENDIX 'B' (*Continued*)

		Villains	Bordars	Serfs	Freemen (F) or Sokemen (S)	Others	Totals	Sum Totals T.R.E.	Sum Totals 1086
Boreham (b)	T.R.E.	—	1	1	—	—	2		
	1086	—	1	—	—	—	1		
Boreham (c)	T.R.E.	—	1	—	—	—	1	53	
	1086	—	1	1	—	—	2		46
Fee of Richeham in *Boreham*	T.R.E.	1	—	1	—	—	2		
	1086	—	2	—	—	—	2		
Walc'fara in *Boreham*	T.R.E.	—	9	8	—	—	17		
	1086	1	15	5	—	—	21		
Kenetuna in *Boreham*	T.R.E.	1	6	3	—	—	10		
	1086	1	4	3	—	—	8		
Broomfield	T.R.E.	9	4	5	—	—	18		
	1086	9	—	4	—	—	13		
Belstead Hall in *Broomfield* (a)	T.R.E.	—	—	2	—	—	2		
	1086	—	—	1	—	—	1		
Belstead Hall in *Broomfield* (b)	T.R.E.	—	3	1	—	—	4		
	1086	—	3	1	—	—	4	36	33
Patching Hall in *Broomfield* (a)	T.R.E.	1	4	1	—	—	6		
	1086	3	4	1	—	—	8		
Patching Hall in *Broomfield* (b)	T.R.E.	—	—	1	—	—	1		
	1086	—	—	1	—	—	1		
Patching Hall in *Broomfield* (c)	T.R.E.	1	4	—	—	—	5		
	1086	—	6	—	—	—	6		
Buttsbury	T.R.E.	6	8	4	—	—	18	22	
	1086	4	12	3	—	—	19		23

APPENDIX 'B' *(Continued)*

		Villains	Bordars	Serfs	Freemen (F) or Sokemen (S)	Others	Totals	Sum Totals T.R.E.	Sum Totals 1086
Festinges in Buttsbury?	T.R.E.	–	3	1	–	–	4		
	1086	–	4	–	–	–	4		
Chelmsford	T.R.E.	5	–	–	–	–	5	5	
	1086	4	–	–	–	–	4		4
Chignal (a)	T.R.E.	–	2	3	3 (F)	–	8		
	1086	3	10	3	–	–	16		
Chignal (b)	T.R.E.	1	1	3	–	–	5		
	1086	1	3	2	–	–	6		
Chignal (c)	T.R.E.	–	3	–	–	–	3		
	1086	–	3	–	–	–	3	22	30
Chignal (d)	T.R.E.	–	–	–	1 (F)	–	1		
	1086	–	–	–	1 (F)	–	1		
Chignal (e)	T.R.E.	–	–	–	1 (F)	1 priest	2		
	1086	–	–	–	1 (F)	–	1		
Chignal Zoyn	T.R.E.	1	2	–	–	–	3		
	1086	1	2	–	–	–	3		
Danbury	T.R.E.	1	3	4	–	–	8	8	
	1086	1	9	1	–	–	11		11
Fryerning? (a)	T.R.E.	1	3	1	–	–	5	6	
	1086	1	9	3	–	–	13		14

APPENDIX 'B' *(Continued)*

		Villains	Bordars	Serfs	Freemen (F) or Sokemen (S)	Others	Totals	Sum Totals T.R.E.	Sum Totals 1086
Fryerning? *(b)*	T.R.E.	–	1	–	–	–	1		
	1086	–	1	–	–	–	1		
Hanningfield, East	T.R.E.	3	–	2	–	–	5	5	11
	1086	–	9	2	–	–	11		
Hanningfield, South *(a)*	T.R.E.	3	2	4	–	–	9	61	66
	1086	3	5	8	–	–	16		
Hanningfield, South *(b)*	T.R.E.	1	18	8	25 (F)	–	52		
	1086	1	18	8	23 (F)	–	50		
Hanningfield, West *(a)*	T.R.E.	–	3	2	–	–	5	7	5
	1086	–	3	2	–	–	5		
Hanningfield West *(b)*	T.R.E.	–	–	2	–	–	2		
	1086	–	–	–	–	–	–		
Hanningfield	T.R.E.	–	–	–	–	–	–	–	2
	1086	–	1	1	–	–	2		
Ingatestone	T.R.E.	2	6	1	–	–	9	9	11
	1086	2	7	1	1 (S)	–	11		
Leighs (Lees) *(a)*	T.R.E.	3	2	7	–	–	12	27	32
	1086	3	9	2	–	–	14		
Leighs (Lees) *(b)*	T.R.E.	4	8	3	–	–	15		
	1086	2	12	4	–	–	18		

APPENDIX 'B' (Continued)

		Villains	Bordars	Serfs	Freemen (F) or Sokemen (S)	Others	Totals	Sum Totals T.R.E.	Sum Totals 1086
Margaretting (a)	T.R.E.	6	3	2	—	—	11	30	29
	1086	6	3	1	—	—	10		
Margaretting (b)	T.R.E.	7	8	4	—	—	19		
	1086	7	8	4	—	—	19		
Moulsham in *Chelmsford*	T.R.E.	8	4	—	—	—	12	12	26
	1086	3	21	2	—	—	26		
Mountnessing? (a)	T.R.E.	18	8	5	—	—	31		
	1086	16	20	7	—	—	43		
Mountnessing? (b)	T.R.E.	—	—	2	2 (F)	—	4	?38	?50
	1086	—	3	1	1 (F)	—	5		
Mountnessing? (c)	T.R.E.	—	—	—	2 (Free maidens)	—	2		
	1086	—	—	—	1 (F)	—	1		
Cowbridge in *Mountnessing*	T.R.E.	—	—	—	1 (F)	—	1		
	1086	—	—	—	1 (F)	—	1		
Rettendon (a)	T.R.E.	26	6	7	—	—	39		
	1086	26	6	6	—	—	38		
Rettendon (b)	T.R.E.	—	4	2	—	—	6	46	45
	1086	—	4	2	—	—	6		
Rettendon (c)	T.R.E.	—	1	—	—	—	1		
	1086	—	1	—	—	—	1		
Runwell (a)	T.R.E.	8	8	2	—	—	18		
							17		

APPENDIX 'B' *(Continued)*

		Villains	Bordars	Serfs	Freemen (F) or Sokemen (S)	Others	Totals	Sum Totals T.R.E.	1086
Runwell *(b)*	T.R.E.	—	2	—	—	—	2		
	1086	—	3	—	—	—	3		
Sandon *(a)*	T.R.E.	1	9	6	—	—	16		
	1086	—	10	1	—	—	11		
Sandon *(b)*	T.R.E.	—	5	—	5 (F)	—	10	38	27
	1086	—	5	—	1 (F)	—	6		
Sandon *(c)*	T.R.E.	2	7	2	1 (F)	—	12		
	1086	—	7	2	1 (F)	—	10		
Springfield *(a)*	T.R.E.	4	7	—	—	—	11		
	1086	4	7	—	—	—	11	30	31
Springfield *(b)*	T.R.E.	6	3	8	2 (F)	—	19		
	1086	4	10	6	—	—	20		
Waltham, Great	T.R.E.	72	28	14	—	—	114		
	1086	72	30	13	3 (F)	—	118		
Alwin's Land in Great Waltham	T.R.E.	3	4	1	—	—	8		
	1086	3	6	1	—	—	10		
Chatham in Great Waltham	T.R.E.	2	2	6	—	—	10	158	171
	1086	2	5	6	—	—	13		
Waltham, Little	T.R.E.	—	4	2	—	—	6		
	1086	—	7	1	—	—	8		
Channels in Little Waltham	T.R.E.	1	7	2	—	—	10		
	1086	1	7	2	—	—	10		

APPENDIX 'B' *(Continued)*

		Villains	Bordars	Serfs	Freemen (F) or Sokemen (S)	Others	Totals	Sum Totals T.R.E.	Sum Totals 1086
Waltham (?Great or Little)	T.R.E.	–	9	1	–	–	10		
	1086	–	11	1	–	–	12		
Widford	T.R.E.	*Not mentioned in Domesday*						–	
	1086								–
Woodham Ferrers	T.R.E.	24	8	6	–	–	38	38	
	1086	24	31	4	–	–	59		59

APPENDIX 'C'

LIBERI TENENTES, 1328

Size of Holding	No. of such Holdings	Services and Obligations
1 carucate	1	Forester of Writtle. Quit rent 33s. 4d.
3 virgates	1	Quit rent 40s.
2½ virgates	1	Suit of court. Maintain 25 perches of park pale. Tallage. Relief. Quit rent part of 6s. 8d.[1]
2 virgates	1	Tallage. Quit rent 20s.
1 virgate	7[2]	(1) Suit of court. Maintain 10p. of park pale. Quit rent 13s. 4d. (2) Totally exempt. (3) Quit rent 6s. 8d. (4) Suit of court. Maintain 10p. of park pale. Tallage. Quit rent 10s. (5) Suit of court. Maintain 10p. of park pale. Quit rent 6s. 8d. (6) Suit of court. Maintain 10p. of park pale. Quit rent 6d. (7) Suit of court. Maintain 10p. of park pale. Heriot. Quit rent 18s. 6d.
½ virgate	9[3]	(1) Quit rent 5s. (2) Suit of court. Maintain 5p. of park pale. Avesage. Tallage. Quit rent 16s. (3) Suit of court. Maintain 5p. of park pale. Avesage. Tallage. Quit rent 8s. (4) Maintain 5p. of park pale. Quit rent 10s. (5) Suit of court. Maintain 5p. of park pale. Avesage. Tallage. Quit rent 7s. 3d. (6) Suit of court. Maintain 5p. of park pale. Tallage. Quit rent 5s. (7) Suit of court. Maintain 5p. of park pale. Tallage. Relief. Quit rent 15s. 8d. (8) Suit of court. Quit rent 5s. (9) Quit rent 12d.
⅓ virgate	1	Suit of court. Maintain 3⅓p. of park pale. Tallage. Relief. Quit rent part of 6s. 8d.
¼ virgate	2	(1) Maintain 2½p. of park pale. Tallage. Quit rent 8s. (2) Suit of court.
31 acres and 1 acre pasture (part of 1 virgate)	1	Suit of court. Proportion of 10p. of park pale. Tallage. Relief. Quit rent part of 6s. 8d.

[1] The 2½ virgates were held jointly with ⅓ virgate, 6 acres part of 1 virgate and a messuage, 31 acres of land and 1 acre of pasture part of 1 virgate (all listed separately below) at a composite quit rent of 6s. 8d.

[2] One virgate also had additionally *vastatum boscum de Radewell'*

[3] One half virgate also had 4 crofts and other unspecified arable, meadow and pasture.

APPENDIX 'C' *(Continued)*

Size of Holding	No. of such Holdings	Services and Obligations
8 acres (part of ½ virgate)	1	Tallage. Quit rent 8d.
8 acres (part of ¼ virgate)	1	Maintain proportion of 2½p. of park pale. Quit rent 2s.
6 acres (part of 1 virgate)	1	Suit of court. Maintain proportion of 10p. of park pale. Tallage. Relief. Quit rent part of 6s. 8d.
4 acres (part of ½ virgate)	1	Maintain proportion of 5p. of park pale. Tallage. Quit rent 2s. 3d.
2½ acres (part of 1 virgate)	1	Maintain proportion of 10p. of park pale. Tallage. Quit rent 15d.
2 acres (part of ½ virgate)	1	Maintain proportion of 5p. of park pale. Tallage. Quit rent 6d.
1 acre of pasture and 3 roods of meadow (part of ½ virgate)	1	Maintain proportion of 5p. of park pale. Tallage. Quit rent 2d.
1 acre of meadow (part of 1 virgate)	1	Maintain proportion of 10p. of park pale. Tallage. Avesage. Heriot. Quit rent 12d.
41 acres	1	Foreign service. Quit rent a pair of gloves worth 1d.
13 acres	1	Quit rent 12d.
11 acres	1	Quit rent 2s.
2 acres	1	Quit rent 9d.
1½ acres	1	Quit rent 12d.
1 acre of meadow	1	Quit rent 6d.
3 roods	1	Tallage. Quit rent 1d.
Unspecified tenement in the vill	1	Quit rent 7s.
Watermill and pasture	1	Quit rent 10s.

APPENDIX 'D'

HOLDINGS BY UNSPECIFIED TENURE

Size	No.	Services and Obligations
1 virgate	1	Maintain 10 perches of park pale.
⅓ virgate	2	(1) Suit of court. Boonworks: 'Bedewedyng' ' and 'Custumbedrepp' '. Maintain 3⅓ p. of park pale. Avesage. Tallage. Quit rent 20*d.* (2) Suit of court. 'Bedewedyng' ', 'Custumbedrepp' ' and 'Molrepp' '. Quit rent 3*s.*
28 acres 1½ roods	1	Maintain 5p. of park pale. Tallage. Heriot. Relief 14*s.* 5*d.* Quit rent 14*s.* 5*d.*
10½ acres, part of ½ virgate	1	Maintain 5p. of park pale with coholders of rest of ½ virgate. Avesage. Heriot. Relief 3*s.* 9*d.* Quit rent 3*s.* 9*d.*
10 acres	1	Maintain 6 furlongs of park pale for all other services and customs.
10 acres (a croft)	1	Heriot. Quit rent 1*d.*
8 acres	1	Tallage. Quit rent 11*d.*
7 acres	1	Avesage. Tallage. Quit rent 15*d.*
3½ acres	1	Suit of court twice a year. Relief 3*s.* Quit rent 3*s.*
3 acres	4	(1) Week work between Lammas Day and Michaelmas as a *foremannus.* Avesage. Tallage. Quit rent 18*d.* and 1 capon at Whitsun. (2) 'Bedewedying' ' and 'Molrepp' '. Quit rent 2*s.*9*d.* and a cock and hen at Christmas. (3) 'Bedewedyng' '. Quit rent 17*d.* and a cock and hen. (4) Avesage. Heriot. Tallage. Relief 15*d.* Quit rent 20*d.*
2½ acres	2	(1) Suit of court. 'Bedewedyng' ', 'Custumbedrepp' ' and 'Molrepp' '. Maintain p. of park pale. Avesage. Heriot. Tallage. Relief 7*d.* (2) Quit rent 10*d.*
2 acres	3	(1) Quit rent 1*d.* (2) Tallage. Quit rent 5½*d.* (3) Avesage. Heriot. Tallage. Relief 15*d.* Quit rent 15*d.*
2 acres, part of ¼ virgate	1	Suit of court. Maintain park pale (with coholders of ¼ virgate). Avesage. Tallage. Quit rent 12*d.*
2 acres of meadow, part of ½ virgate	1	Quit rent 2*s.*

APPENDIX 'D' *(Continued)*

Size	No.	Services and Obligations
2 acres of pasture	1	Quit rent 2s.
1 acre	2	(1) Quit rent a cock and a hen. (2) Quit rent 6d.
Messuage	1	Tallage. Quit rent 10½d.
Cottage	1	Quit rent a cock and a hen.
Smithy	1	Quit rent 2d.
Purprestures	8	(1) – (6) 1d.; (7) – (8) 2d.

APPENDIX 'E'

GRAIN ACCOUNT, MICHAELMAS 1360–MICHAELMAS 1361[1]

Grain	Stock Held	qrs.	bus.	p.
Wheat	Left over (from 1359 harvest)	3	3	0
(threshed)	From 1360 harvest	213	7	3
	From farm of watermill	6	0	0
	First receipt of threshed grain from 1361 harvest	27	0	0
		250	2	3
	Issues			
	Sown for 1361 harvest	69	6	0
	Allowances of the *famuli*	5	6	3
	Bread for 96 reapers	1	0	0
	To Wm. Halford, woodward of Highwood	1	0	0
	Sold to the lord's household	39	0	0
	Sold to merchants	30	0	0
	Merchants' profit	1	4	0
	Given to Friars of Chelmsford	1	0	0
	Part of payment to carpenter contracting to repair byre at Boyton	0	1	0
	Part of payment to carpenter contracting to repair Brixebregg	0	1	0
		149	2	3

Surplus: 101 qrs. for seed (erroneously given as 51 qrs. in the account)

	Stock Held	qrs.	bus.	p.
Maslin	Left over (from 1359 harvest)	10	0	0
(threshed)	From 1360 harvest	12	4	2
		22	4	2
	Issues			
	Sown for 1361 harvest	10	0	0
	Sold to the lord's household	9	0	0
	Allowances of the *famuli*	1	4	2
		20	4	2

Surplus: 2 qrs.

[1] E.R.O., D/DP M559.

APPENDIX 'E' *(Continued)*

	Stock Held	qrs.	bus.	p.
Peas	Left over (from 1359 harvest)	6	5	0
(threshed)	From 1360 harvest	5	2	0
		11	7	0
	Issues			
	Sown for 1361 harvest	5	2	0
	Sold upon the account	6	5	0
		11	7	0

Surplus: None.

	Stock Held	qrs.	bus.	p.
Barley	From 1360 harvest	63	4	0
(threshed)				
	Issues			
	Sown for 1361 harvest	16	2	0
	Mixed with oats for drage (see below)	2	0	0
	Sold to merchants	43	0	0
	Merchants' profit	2	1	2
	Sold upon the account	0	0	2
		63	4	0

Surplus: None.

	Stock Held	qrs.	bus.	p.
Drage	From 1360 harvest (2 qrs. of oats and 2 qrs. of	14	4	0
(threshed)	barley received for mixing after Michaelmas 1360)			
	Issues			
	Sown for 1361 harvest	4	0	0
	Provender for the horses	2	0	0
	Sold to merchants	7	5	0
	Merchants' profit	0	3	0
	Sold upon the account	0	4	0
		14	4	0

Surplus: None.

APPENDIX 'E' *(Continued)*

	Stock Held	qrs.	bus.	p.
Benemong	From 1360 harvest	14	2	0
(threshed)	? Left over from 1359 harvest	2	3	2
		16	5	2

	Issues			
	Sown for 1361 harvest	14	2	0
	Sold upon the account	2	3	2
		16	5	2

Surplus: None.

	Stock Held			
Bolymong	From 1360 harvest	17	6	0
(threshed)	? (source not given)		2	0
		18	0	0

	Issues			
	Sown for 1361 harvest	5	0	0
	Sold to lord's household	12	6	0
	Sold on the account		2	0
		18	0	0

Surplus: None.

	Stock Held			
Oats	From 1360 harvest (threshed)	260	6	0
	Held for drage	2	0	0
	Held for drage (estimated quantity of 78 shocks)	9	6	0
		272	4	0

APPENDIX 'E' *(Continued)*

Issues	qrs.	bus.	p.
Sown for 1361 harvest	79	0	0
Mixed with barley for drage (see above)	2	0	0
Flour made for potage of *famuli*	4	0	0
Provender of 4 cart horses	11	0	0
Provender of 24 stotts and of 4 cart horses hired for 28 days for the 5th additional plough	38	2	0
Provender of 16 oxen (66 shocks)	8	2	0
Sustaining weak cows (4 shocks)	0	2	0
At weaning of calves and lambs	0	7	0
Provender of horses of John de Chertes the constable coming to hold courts and to supervise the manor	1	2	0
Sold to lord's household	123	0	0
Sold on the account	4	5	0
	272	4	0

Surplus: None.

APPENDIX 'F'

ACCOUNT OF 'WORKS', 1360–61

		Winter 'Works' (30 Sept.–28 March)

'Shokm(anni)' (Custumarii Operarii)

Nominal total due from 18¼ virgates		2,281¼
Less for feastdays and 'Gaueldays' before Christmas		529¼
Less for ½ virgate and two ¼ virgates 'at farm'		128
		657¼
Total deductions	657¼	
Total remaining	1,624	

Akermanni and Formanni

Nominal total due from 7²/₃ virgates		1,153
Less for feastdays		161
Less works of two *akermanni* serving as beadle and ploughman and two *formanni* serving as shepherds and cowherds		176
Less works of two ¹/₃ virgates of *formanni* 'at farm'		88
		425
Total deductions	425	
Total remaining	728	

Total of works due from the *shokmanni, akermanni* and *formanni* after above deductions	2,352	
Less works sold (from which tenures not distinguished)	872½	
Remainder = works performed	1,479½	

APPENDIX 'F' *(Continued)*

		Summer 'Works' (29 Mar.–24 June)	
'Shokm(anni) (Custumarii Operarii)			
Nominal total due from 18¼ virgates		1,099	
Less for feastdays and 'Gaueldays' before Christmas			182½
Less for ½ virgate and two ¼ virgates 'at farm'			64
			246½
	Total deductions	246½	
	Total remaining	852½	
Akermanni and Formanni			
Nominal total due from 7⅔ virgates		555	
Less for feastdays			69
Less works of two *akermanni* serving as beadle and ploughman and two *formanni* serving as shepherds and cowherds			100
Less works of two ⅓ virgates of *formanni* 'at farm'			50
			219
	Total deductions	219	
	Total remaining	336	
Total of works due from the *Shokmanni, Akermanni* and *Formanni* after above deductions		1,188½	
Less works sold (from which tenures not distinguished)		568 5/12	
	Remainder = works performed	620 1/12	

APPENDIX 'F' *(Continued)*

	Autumn 'Works' (25 June–29 Sept.)	
Shokm(anni) (Custumarii Operarii)		
Nominal total due from 18¼ virgates	1,190¼	
Less for feastdays and 'Gaueldays' before Christmas		182½
Less for ½ virgate and two ¼ virgates 'at farm'		69
		251½
Total deductions	251½	
Total remaining	938¾	
Akermanni and Formanni		
Nominal total due from 7⅔ virgates	604	
Less for feastdays		–
Less works of two *akermanni* serving as beadle and ploughman and two *formanni* serving as shepherds and cowherds		112
Less works of two ⅓·virgates of *formanni* 'at farm'		56
		168
Total deductions	168	
Total remaining	436	
Total of works due from the *shokmanni, akermanni* and *formanni* after above deductions	1,374¾	
Less works sold (from which tenures not distinguished)	317	
Remainder = works performed	1,057¾	

APPENDIX 'G'

LIVESTOCK ACCOUNT, 1360–1

	At 30 Sept. 1360	Additions	Losses	At 29 Sept. 1361
Cart horses	4 (2 weak)	–	–	4 (2 weak)
Stotts	26 (3 weak)	2 (by purchase)	2 (murrain)	26 (4 weak)
Oxen	16	2 (from heriots)	2 (old, sold)	16
Bulls	1	–	–	1
Cows	60	3 (from heifers below)	1 (unjustly taken for heriot, returned)	
		1 (by purchase)	2 (old, sold)	
		4 (from heriots)	1 (from heriots, weak, sold)	64
Bullocks	3	–	3 (sold)	–
Heifers	3	–	3 (transferred to cows above)	–
Steers	6	–	–	6
Calves (year-old)	8	–		8 steers
Calves (new born)	–	8 (purchased from the farmer of the cows)	–	8 year-old calves
Rams	9	–	1 (murrain, before shearing)	8
Ewes	208	41 (from the gimmers)	3 (murrain, before lambing and shearing)	
		1 (heriot, after shearing)	3 (murrain, after lambing and before shearing)	
		1 (heriot, after lambing and shearing)	1 (after lambing and shearing)	
		1 (stray, after shearing)	30 (sold)	
			4 (sold upon the account)	211

APPENDIX 'G' *(Continued)*

	At 30 Sept. 1360	Additions	Losses	At 29 Sept. 1361
Sheep	32	17 (from 2nd-year sheep below)	2 (murrain, before shearing)	
			5 (slaughtered for feeding steward and lord's council before shearing)	
			8 (to Bailiff of Foulness)	
			20 (sold after shearing)	
			1 (sold upon the account)	13
2nd-year sheep and gimmers	97 (whereof 80 gimmers)	–	17 (transferred to sheep above)	
			41 (transferred to ewes above)	
			39 (to Reeve of Waltham by 1 tally)	–
Lambs (year-old)	150	80 (from 'le Roos' in Dec. by 1 tally)	45 (murrain, before shearing)	
			110 (to Bailiff of Foulness)	75 2nd-year sheep and gimmers
Lambs (new born)	–	206 (and not more, because 7 'stil'	10 (murrain, before weaning)	
			19 (in tithe)	
		140 (from Reeve of Waltham)	12 (murrain, after weaning)	
			1 (to shepherd as his 'Markyng Lamb')	304 year-old lambs
Pigs	21 (whereof 2 sows)	–	1 (murrain)	
			1 (slaughtered for feeding steward and lord's council in London on lord's business)	

APPENDIX 'G' *(Continued)*

	At 30 Sept. 1360	Additions	Losses	At 29 Sept. 1361
			12 (sold to lord's house-hold)	7 (whereof 1 boar and 2 sows)
Pigs (year-old)	8	7 (from piglets below)	1 (slaughtered for feeding steward as above)	
			7 (sold)	7
Piglets	7	28 (new-born)	3 (in tithe)	
			7 (murrain)	
			7 (transferred to year-old pigs above)	
			2 (sold upon the account)	9
Geese	8 (whereof 2 ganders)	1 (by purchase)	1 (sold upon the account)	2 ganders and 6 geese
Cocks	2	–	–	2
Hens	15	–	–	15

Hides, Wool and Skins

	At 30 Sept. 1360	Additions	Losses	At 29 Sept. 1361
Hides	2 (stotts which died of murrain)	–	1 (sold upon the account)	1 bleached hide
Fleeces	–	445	44½ (in tithe)	
			15 (sold upon the account because they were unshorn owing to weakness)	385½
Wool-fells	–	54 (as a result of murrain)	6 (in tithe)	
		5 (from sheep slaughtered for delivery to London)		53
Small and very small sheepskins	1 small and 10 very small (from murrain)	–	1 very small (in tithe)	10 small and very small

ORIGINAL SOURCES CONSULTED

AND

BIBLIOGRAPHY

ORIGINAL SOURCES CONSULTED

MANORIAL RECORDS

	Reference
Manor of Writtle	
Court rolls, 1379–1793	E.R.O., D/DP M189–417
Court books, 1741–1917	D/DP M418–420, 1452–4
Court minutes, 1736–1938	D/DP M1455–67
Extent, 1328	D/DP M540
Extent, 1419	D/DP M546
Survey, 1548	D/DP M547
Survey, 1564	D/DP M548
Survey, 1594–5	D/DP M549
Compoti, 1360–1, 1376–7, 1404, 1417–8, 1421–2, 1422–32, 1439–59, 1463–8, 1471–4, 1477–8, 1492–3, 1502–3, 1510–11	D/DP M559–594
Custumal, *c.*1580	D/DP M552
Avesage roll, 1377	D/DP M538
Terrier, 1894	D/DP M1474A
Manor of Fithlers in Writtle	
Court rolls, 1654, 1728–1747	D/DP M609–611
Rental, 1700	D/DP M612
Manor of Wallextons in Writtle	
Rentals, 1458–1478	D/DP M613–620
Manor of Moor Hall	
Court papers, 1619	D/DP M623
Manor of Romans Fee in Writtle	
Court rolls, 1584, 1617–1638	New College, Oxford. (Microfilm in E.R.O., T/A 126)
Manor of Newland Fee (or Hall) in Roxwell	
Court rolls, 1448–1606	D/DU 497/28–9
Manor of Mountneys in Roxwell	
Abstracts of court rolls, 1351–1377 (made *c.*1575)	D/DP M622
Manor of Skreens	
Court rolls, 1628, 1636, 1720, 1750	D/DU 497/22–25
Rentals, 1659, 1703	D/DU 497/26, 27

Reference

Manor of Tyehall in Roxwell

Extract from court roll, 1375 — D/DP M621

Abstract of court rolls, 1394−1405 (made *c.*1575) — D/DP M622

Manor of Newarks in Good Easter

Court rolls, 1527−1889 — D/DSp M1−13

Rentals, 1441−1768 — D/DSp M19−30

Survey, 1597 — D/DSp M31

MAPS AND AWARDS

Manor of Newarks in Good Easter, 1620 — D/DSp P1

Manor of Skreens in Roxwell, 1635 — D/DGe P3

Youngs Farm in Roxwell, 1682 (photograph) — T/M 280

Montpeliers Farm in Writtle, 1739 — Wadham College, Oxford (photograph in E.R.O., T/M 304)

Petre family estates in Writtle and Roxwell, 1783 — D/DP P35

Tithe Map and Award of Roxwell, 1842 — D/CT 301

Tithe Map and Award of Writtle, 1843 — D/CT 414

Enclosure Map and Award of Writtle and Roxwell, 1871 — Q/RDc 68

OTHER RECORDS

Charter of King John to Church of St Paul and Bishop of London of market, etc., at Chelmsford, 1199 (certified copy, 1650) — D/DM T28/1

Charters relating to the Manor of Montpeliers in Writtle, early 13th century−1486 (transcribed by C. R. Cheney, typescript copy in E.R.O. (T/A 139) — Wadham College

Charter of land in Writtle, 1298 — E.R.O., D/DP T1/1770

Charter Roll, 5 John (1203−4) — P.R.O.

Extent of Manor of Writtle, 1304 — P.R.O., C.133/113(1)

Pipe Roll 169, 17 Edw. II (1323−4) — P.R.O.

Inquisition post mortem of Alianora de Waleys, 1331 — E.R.O., D/DP T18

Poll Tax Returns for Chelmsford and Writtle, 1377 — P.R.O., E.179/107/46

Survey of Duke of Buckingham's lands, 1521 — E.36/150

BIBLIOGRAPHY

Primary Printed Sources

Annales Monasterii de Burmundeseia (Rolls Series, 1886)
Cartularium Monasterii Sancti Johannis Baptiste de Colcestria (ed. S. A. Moore, 1897)
Early Charters of St Paul's Cathedral (ed. Marion Gibbs, Camden Third Series, vol. lviii, 1939)
Book of Fees, Part I, 1198–1242
Calendar of Charter Rolls, 1257–1300, vol. ii
Calendar of Close Rolls, (volumes as cited in footnotes)
Calendar of Patent Rolls, (volumes as cited in footnotes)
Curia Regis Rolls, vol. ii, 1201–1203
Feet of Fines for Essex, (Essex Archaeological Society), vol. i
Pipe Roll, 14 Hen. III (Pipe Roll Society, New Series 4, 1927)
Pipe Roll, 4 John (P.R.S., New Series 15, 1937)
Pipe Roll, 6 John (P.R.S., New Series 18, 1940)
Pipe Roll, 13 John (P.R.S., New Series 28, 1951–2)

'Calendar of Essex Assize Files, 1559–1714' (typescript, Essex Record Office)
'Calendar of Essex Quarter Session Rolls, 1555–1714' (typescript, E.R.O.)

Secondary Printed Sources

Ault, W. O., 'Village Assemblies in Medieval England' (*Studies presented to the International Commission for the History of Representative and Parliamentary Institutions*, vol. xxiii, Louvain U.P., 1960)
Bennett, H. S., *Life of the English Manor, 1150–1400* (Cambridge, 1938)
Bracton, *De Legibus*
Cromarty, Dorothy, *The Fields of Saffron Walden in 1400* (E.R.O. Publications, No. 43, 1966)
Cam, H. M., *The Hundred and the Hundred Rolls* (Cambridge, 1930)
Camden, W., *Britannia . . .* (1586, 1st English Edition by Philemon Holland, 1610)
Complete Peerage, vol. ii
Coulton, G. C., *Old England*
Darby, H. C., *The Domesday Geography of Eastern England* (Cambridge, 1952)
Essex Field Club, *Transactions*, vol. ii (1882)
Fisher, W. R., *The Forest of Essex* (London, 1887)
Foster, C. W., and Langley, T., *The Lincolnshire Domesday and the Lindsey Survey* (Preface by F. M. Stenton)
Fowler, G. H., *Bedford in 1086: An Analysis and Synthesis of Domesday Book* (Quarto Memoirs of the Bedfordshire Historical Record Society, vol. i, 1922)
Gray, H. L., *English Field Systems* (1915)
Homans, G. C., *English Villagers in the Thirteenth Century* (Cambridge, Mass., 1941)
Hoyt, R. S., *The Royal Demesne in English Constitutional History: 1066–1272* (The American Historical Association, Ithaca, New York, 1950)

Krause, J., 'The Medieval Household: Large or Small?' (*Economic History Review,* 2nd series, vol. x, 1957)

Lamond, E., (ed.) *Walter of Henley's Husbandry* . . . (Royal Historical Society, 1890)

Levett, A. E., *Studies in Manorial History* (Oxford, 1938)

Maitland, F. W., *Select Pleas in Manorial and Other Seignorial Courts* (Selden Society, vol. ii, 1889)

Morant, P., *History of Essex* (1768)

Newton, K. C., *Thaxted in the Fourteenth Century* (E.R.O. Publications, No. 33, 1960)

Orwin, C. S. and C. S., *The Open Fields* (1938)

Pavry, F. H.. and Knocker, G. M., 'The Mount, Princes Risborough' (*Records of Buckinghamshire,* 1957–8)

Pollock, F., and Maitland, F. W., *The History of English Law before the Time of Edward I* (2nd edition, Cambridge, 1923)

Postan, M. M., 'Some Economic Evidence of Declining Population in the Later Middle Ages' (*Economic History Review,* 2nd series, vol. ii, 1950); (with J. Titow) 'Heriots and Prices on Winchester Manors' (*ibid.,* 2nd series, vol. xi, 1958–59); and 'Note' (*ibid.,* 2nd series, vol. xii, 1959–60)

Rahtz, P. A., *Excavations at King John's Hunting Lodge, Writtle, Essex, 1955–57* (Society for Medieval Archaeology Monograph Series: No. 3, 1969)

Reaney, P. H., *Place-Names of Essex* (English Place-Name Society, vol. xii, 1935)

Round, J. H., *Feudal England* (London, 1909)

Royal Commission on Historical Monuments, *Inventory,* Essex, vols. i–iv, (1916–23)

Russell, J. C., *British Medieval Population* (Albuquerque, 1948)

Stow, J., *Annales* (Howes edition, 1631)

Thirsk, Joan, 'The Common Fields' (*Past and Present,* No. 29, 1964)

Thresh, J. C., *Report on the Water Supply in the Village of Writtle in the Chelmsford Rural Sanitary District,* N.D. (*c.* 1890)

Tupling, G. H., 'Markets and Fairs in Medieval Lancashire' (*Essays in Honour of James Tait,* 1933)

Turner, G. J., *Select Pleas of the Forest* (Selden Society, vol. xiii, 1899)

Victoria County History, Essex, vol. i (1907), vol. iii (1963)

Vinogradoff, P., *The Growth of the Manor* (London, 1905)

GENERAL INDEX